I0167803

LITTLE
PROFESSORS

LIFE LESSONS

LEARNED FROM

CHILDREN

DR. TIM KING

Copyright © 2018 by Tim King
Little Professors: Life Lessons Learned from Children / Dr. Tim King

ISBN: 978-1-947671-42-3

All rights reserved. This book or any portion thereof may not be reproduced or used in any manner whatsoever without the express written permission of the author except for the use of brief quotations in a book review.

All Scripture quotations not otherwise designated are taken from the Holy Bible, New International Version®, NIV® Copyright ©1973, 1978, 1984, 2011 by Biblica, Inc.® Used by permission. All rights reserved worldwide.
Scripture quotations marked KJV are from the King James Version of the Bible.

Cover and Interior Design:
D.E. West, ZAQ Designs / Dust Jacket Creative Services

Printed in the United States of America

To my children: Kyler Timothy, McKala Mary, and Kaleigh Rae. They have taught me, they continue to teach me, and they motivate me always to stay in the modality of learning and seeking truth. I love you more than words can express. To my wife, Stacy Lynn: I am forever grateful for these three little professors you gave me with whom to do life. I love you more.

CONTENTS

F O R E W O R D

Tim King has prepared a charming family book that tells stories of how God is working through his children. In each of the fifty-two stories, he reflects on how the Lord was working in his children and through his wife and his ministry.

These stories are not sensational like some nursery rhymes or tell of a missionary family being delivered from persecution or attacks. These stories reflect King's everyday life with his family – like my children when I was much younger, or your children. King describes incidents so normal, that if they happen to your children you may miss the life-long impact that a simple conversation can have in the development of your children.

And yet, every normal incident reflects the life changing power of God, working in ordinary ways, to make a lasting influence on children. As you read each story, study carefully the attached Bible verse. It contains deep truth. These are the truths that you must communicate to your children.

These stories remind me of a lagoon in Hawaii where my family and I visited on a boat trip. "The bottom appears to be only a few feet down," the guide explained. Then he challenged us, "But it is over 100 feet deep . . . dive in and you will not hit the bottom." Isn't that true of God's principles? They seem so simple—on the surface—yet they represent the depth of an enteral God dealing with us.

So, my advice is to dive in and enjoy these stories. And when you and your children do, begin applying these truths and you will find their meanings are as limitless as the promises of God.

Elmer L. Towns
Co-Founder and Vice President, Liberty University

INTRODUCTION

I began this book many years prior to its completion, but for many reasons, including completing a doctoral degree and probably some other priorities as well, this book took many years to finish. Upon completing my doctoral program in clinical counseling--some would say that a Ph.D. program is the pinnacle of higher learning--the thought occurred to me that some of the greatest lessons I have ever learned came straight from the mouths of babes, namely my own children. Have you ever heard that all you ever need to know you could learn in kindergarten? There's certainly a whole lot of truth to that statement.

This book, however, is suggesting that you can begin to learn from children even before kindergarten and continue to learn from them throughout their life spans as well. As a matter of fact, children can teach you from their birth to kindergarten and beyond if you're listening to the still, small voice of their Creator.

Being a parent is no doubt one of the greatest blessings and toughest jobs ever given to humanity. I can remember when my wife and I decided to start our family after being married for just a few years. We would be driving down the road and tell our children (who did not exist yet) to be quiet in the back seat of the car. We would tell our son to stop picking on his sister. We would tell them to use their inside voices. I'm sure the people in the cars beside us and behind us were wondering how this hallucinating couple got their driver's licenses. Talk about the power of the spoken word! We later would call Kyler, McKala, and Kaleigh our own.

I have a dream that all who read this book of life lessons taught by my children would begin to listen intently to the truths that come from the mouths of babes. Each story is accompanied by a Scripture verse, as all principled truth is either scientific or scriptural and originates with God. The book contains fifty-two stories, one for each week of the year. The intention is that the reader will take one story and meditate on it for the week.

All of us want to be better in the roles we've been given. I assure you that reading, meditating on, and applying these truths taught by my very own little professors of life will indeed motivate you to new heights in your various roles. I have left the children's spelling errors in the stories. Enjoy reading. Class is in!

McKala, Kaleigh, and Kyler King

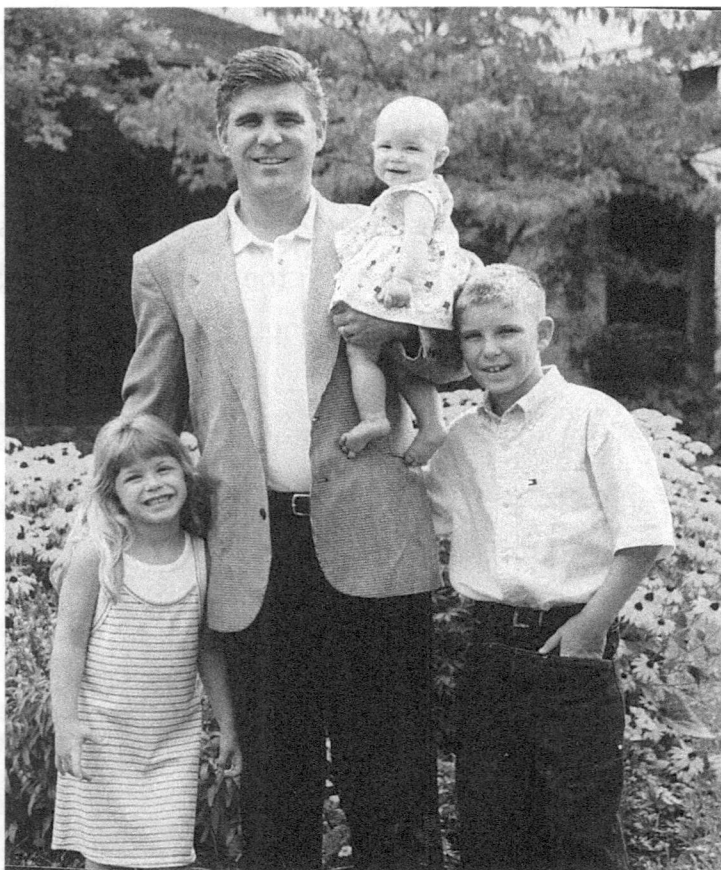

McKala, Dad holding Kaleigh, and Kyler

WEEK ONE

(New Year's Day)

In the beginning was the Word,
and the Word was with God,
and the Word was God.
(John 1:1)

IT ALL BEGINS WITH JESUS, THE SON OF GOD

10-9-8-7-6-5-4-3-2-1. Balloons, whistles, and all kinds of other noise-making gadgets. Something is about to happen--a new year! How many hundreds of millions of people all over the world count down the end of one year to usher in the beginning of a new year? We have done this every year with our children.

At one particular New Year's Day dinner my daughter McKala said a prayer that included this phrase:

"Thank You, God, for a new year to spend with You and family and friends." New beginnings, new goals, and new year's resolutions are all part of the onset of a new year. It is important to remember that our time here on earth is but a vapor--it appears for just a little while and then vanishes away. "Why, you do not even know what will happen tomorrow. What is your life? You are a mist that appears for a little while and then vanishes" (James 4:14).

So many of us put all our effort and energy into accumulating stuff during the short time that we are here on earth and so little time investing into eternity. We have taught our children, and yes, they have taught us, that we have an opportunity to invest in eternity. McKala's prayer was thanking God for a new year to carve out some time to spend with Him. Making this time to develop and deepen your relationship with your Creator is one of the most important things you can do with your time in any year, let alone the coming new year. Spending time with family and friends whom we can bring to heaven with us is also a top priority and a blessing from God.

Scripture tells us that God was there in the very beginning of your time clock and that He is the taker of life and therefore is at the end of your time clock here on earth. God is not bound to a big clock in New York City, for He is eternal. Scripture tells us that a thousand years in heaven is like one minute to God.

Let me encourage you as my daughter McKala encouraged us. Make this new year one in which you spend time with the Creator of the universe and also spend some time with family and friends who have the opportunity to hang out with you and Jesus through-out all eternity.

PRINCIPLE FOR LIVING:

Spend your days on earth living
with eternity in mind.

WEEK TWO

*Do you not know that in a race all
the runners run, but only one gets the prize?
Run in such a way as to get the prize.*
(1 Corinthians 9:24)

AND THE WINNER IS . . .?

I have heard many countless prayers in my life as a Christian. I have heard noble men pray. I have heard presidents of universities pray. I have heard famous celebrities pray. I have to tell you that the greatest, most potent prayers I've ever heard have come from the mouths of children and many of those prayers from the mouths of my own children.

We as a family often bow our heads and join hands to thank God for His provision before we eat a meal in our home. It is one of the practices that I learned from my mom and dad when I was a kid. On one particular dinner occasion Kyler led our family in prayer. I must confess that I was expecting a simple, short "Thank You for this food" prayer, because all our family had expressed how hungry we were. Prior to dinner Kyler was showing us a participation ribbon, he had received at church in a children's program called AWANA, where they play games and learn truths from the Word of God. They also had distributed prizes for various accomplishments in this particular children's church program.

Kyler had not received a prize as had many of the other kids. What came out of his mouth as a child pierced the heart of his mother and me. He began to pray, "Dear Jesus, thank You for this food, and it's okay that I didn't get a prize at AWANA because I have You, Jesus, and You're the best prize anyone could ever have. Amen."

Kyler had somehow understood that the winner of life's race is the one who receives the prize of knowing Jesus.

PRINCIPLE FOR LIVING:

Seek to know Jesus if you want to win in life.

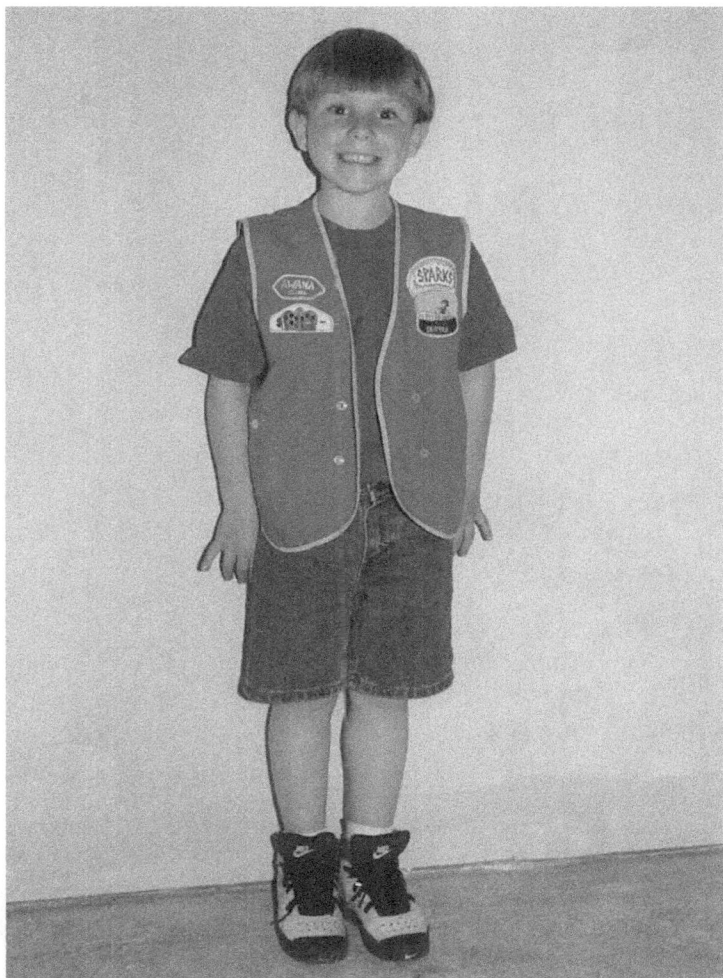

Kyler in his AWANA uniform

WEEK THREE

"The grass withers and the flowers fall, because the breath of the Lord blows on them. Surely the people are grass. The grass withers and the flowers fall, but the word of our God endures forever." You who bring good news to Zion, go up on a high mountain. You who bring good news to Jerusalem, lift up your voice with a shout, lift it up, do not be afraid; say to the towns of Judah, "Here is your God!" See, the Sovereign LORD comes with power, and he rules with a mighty arm. See, his reward is with him, and his recompense accompanies him. He tends his flock like a shepherd: He gathers the lambs in his arms and carries them close to his heart; he gently leads those that have young. Who has measured the waters in the hollow of his hand, or with the breadth of his hand marked off the heavens? Who has held the

dust of the earth in a basket, or weighed the
mountains on the scales and the hills in a balance?
Who can fathom the Spirit of the LORD, or
instruct the LORD as his counselor?
(Isaiah 40:7-13)

HOW BIG IS YOUR GOD?

This is about a life lesson that came from the song "Lord, I Lift Your Name on High." After singing this song, my daughter Kaleigh asked this question: "Dad, can you lift God?" It was my opportunity to explain to her the enormity of our God--not the easiest task a dad can have but one that is worthy of our time. I began using the analogies the prophet Isaiah used in Isaiah 40 to try to explain to her little mind how enormous God really is. He is certainly bigger than any problem you or I can ever have.

Isaiah notes the size of God by comparing the size of a human being to that of a single blade of grass. He goes on to explain that God can hold the waters of the world in the palm of His hand. He talks about how God just blows a puff of air and rearranges the mountains.

If you are currently experiencing any kind of problem, big or small, it would be well worth it to read Isaiah 40. Once I explained Isaiah's description of how big God is to my daughter, she was able to conclude in her own mind that her dad couldn't come close to lifting God. However, you and I on a regular basis can lift the name of Jesus in adoration, on high as the song so eloquently says. (More to come about this song in a later chapter.)

PRINCIPLE FOR LIVING:

Giving your problem to God always shrinks the size of the problem.

W E E K   F O U R

The LORD himself goes before you and will be with you;
he will never leave you nor forsake you.
Do not be afraid; do not be discouraged.
(Deuteronomy 31:8)

NO NEED TO FEEL LONELY

There are times in our life when we inevitably fall into the feeling of being lonely. There are times in all my children's lives when they have reported to their mother and me that they felt lonely. It might have been that they were not included in an invitation to a party, or maybe they were the last one to be chosen on a team at a ball game, or maybe they were alone without friends on a snow day.

Whatever the circumstance, we have all felt lonely at times. I can remember telling my daughter McKala about one such time for me, a time when you would never expect a person to feel lonely--since I was sitting in a sea of forty thousand men. It was a gathering of men in a football stadium attending a Promise Keepers conference. I had traveled to this conference with a group of men from a church I did not attend.

Upon arrival at the stadium, all these men began grouping together and heading off to find seats in the packed stadium. I was unable to locate the men I was to meet at this conference--and ended up sitting by myself for the first session of the conference.

I was able to explain to McKala that God, the Father of all fathers, has promised never to leave us and never to forsake us and that there is no place we can go to get away from His love. That is a very comforting thought and promise from God when we're feeling lonely.

There are times in every parent's life where we wish we could accompany our children, and yet we send them off to an athletic camp for a week, a church camp for a week, a cross-cultural mission trip, and ultimately off to college. It is a great comfort when you give them that last hug and kiss them goodbye that they are never truly alone. This God, who promised never to leave us or forsake us, is capable of looking past the universe, past the earth, past the 325 million people who inhabit the United States of America, past the state you live in, past the county you live in, and past the city or town you live in and to focus his energy upon one single person--and that person is you. You are never alone.

PRINCIPLE FOR LIVING:

You are never truly alone when you acknowledge the presence of God.

WEEK FIVE

Trust in the Lord with all your heart and lean
not on your own understanding; in all your ways submit
to him, and he will make your paths straight.
(Proverbs 3:5-6)

WHO DO YOU TRUST?

On May 19, 2005, while riding in the car with my four-year-old daughter, Kaleigh, after taking my parents to breakfast, I said to her, "Is your tummy full?"

Kaleigh replied, "Yes, my tummy is full."

I then told her, "Be sure to thank Jesus for your pancakes, because all good things come from Him."

Kaleigh then said in her innocent, childlike voice, "What does Jesus do if He gets hungry?"

My reply to her, knowing that there's fruit in heaven, was that He probably eats fruit.

She then replied, "Daddy, Attie [our golden retriever dog that had died about a year prior] is in heaven with Jesus, and I bet you if Jesus tells Attie to sit that she listens to Him and sits."

I pondered this childlike faith and replied to my daughter, "I bet you too that Attie Girl does listen to Jesus, and I hope you and I listen to Jesus too."

Are you in total submission to God? Who is in the driver's seat of your life? In chapter 18 of the Book of Luke Jesus asks His listeners a question: "Are you willing to sell all you have and follow me?" (Luke 18:22, author's translation) Are you totally surrendered to the point that if Jesus told you to sit, stand, run, jump, or anything else, you would in total childlike faith sell all you have and obey Him?

PRINCIPLE FOR LIVING:

Put your total trust in God alone.

McKala, Tim, Stacy, and Kyler with Attie and her 11 puppies

WEEK SIX

*For we know that if the earthly tent we live in
is destroyed, we have a building from God, an
eternal house in heaven, not built by human hands.
Meanwhile we groan, longing to be clothed
instead with our heavenly dwelling.*
(2 Corinthians 5:1-2)

SO, YOU WANT A NEW BODY?

I have been blessed with many ministry opportunities in my life. One was as the director of a ministry outreach team that used karate as a method to communicate truth. Now make no mistake about it: I am no Bruce Lee or Texas Walker Ranger. As a matter of fact, when I was asked to be the director of this outreach team, I had never taken a karate lesson in my life.

Things were about to change! I am proud to say that at the conclusion of this leadership experience, I had obtained my yellow belt in karate. And yes, my yellow belt has blood on it to prove to all that I was bad to the bone. Well, in reality it was *my* blood on the yellow belt and I was really *not* bad to the bone in karate.

I did, however, receive a karate lesson from my son, Kyler, who was about four years of age at the time. It came on a day when I was putting my ghee on and tying my yellow belt around the ghee. Kyler looked at me with his matter-of-fact eyes and said boldly, "Hey, Dad--you know there will be no karate in heaven!"

My response was "Oh, yeah? What makes you say that, Kyler?"

Kyler proceeded to inform his dad with his theological expertise that the Bible says that nobody gets hurt in heaven. Can you imagine? The Bible tells us that when we pass from this life into the next and we know God's Son, Jesus Christ, as our personal Lord and Savior, we will have new heavenly bodies. There are all kinds of theological discussions about this but suffice it to say that whatever this body in heaven will look like, it does not get sick, injured, or feel pain.

What a joyful truth when we see the sicknesses and injuries that our bodies here on earth experience! No more migraine headaches, no more sports injuries, no more dreaded diseases. Kyler's truth that day just reminds us of the many glorious things we have to look forward to on the other side of this earth.

PRINCIPLE FOR LIVING:

On this earth, pain in your body is a reminder of the new body you can look forward to.

Tim in his karate gi

WEEK SEVEN

(Valentine's Day)

*A new command I give you: Love one another.
As I have loved you, so you must love one
another. By this everyone will know that you
are my disciples, if you love one another.*
(John 13:34-35)

WHAT IS IN YOUR HEART?

More wisdom from Kaleigh at age 6 written on a birthday card to me. Kaleigh writes, "Remember your wish is in your hart [heart], your family." Scripture admonishes us to guard our hearts, for out of it springs the issues of life (Proverbs 4:23). Hopefully one of the issues of your heart is your family.

Kaleigh writes, "Happy 80th birthday dad [What? I was only 48!]. I love you and I think you are the best hunter in the world. I appsolooty [absolutely] love hunting with you. Thank you so much for taking care of me and loving me. You are speishal [special] to me and to God. God loves you and I hope you have the greatest birthday ever! You are the best dad in the whole wide world. I think you have the biggest hart [heart] to take time to help people like me."

How much time have you carved out in your calendar for family this week? Someone once said that a relationship is based upon three words: "time spent with." Some of my fondest memories are being in the woods hunting with my children. In a world where everything is calling for our attention, we need to make sure that we carve out time to deepen our relationships with our family members. Know this for sure– God thinks you are special, and He longs to spend time with you daily. He wants you to deepen your relationships with family by choosing to spend time with them.

PRINCIPLE FOR LIVING:

The greatest motivation for good on earth is
to understand God's love for us and
to point others to that love.

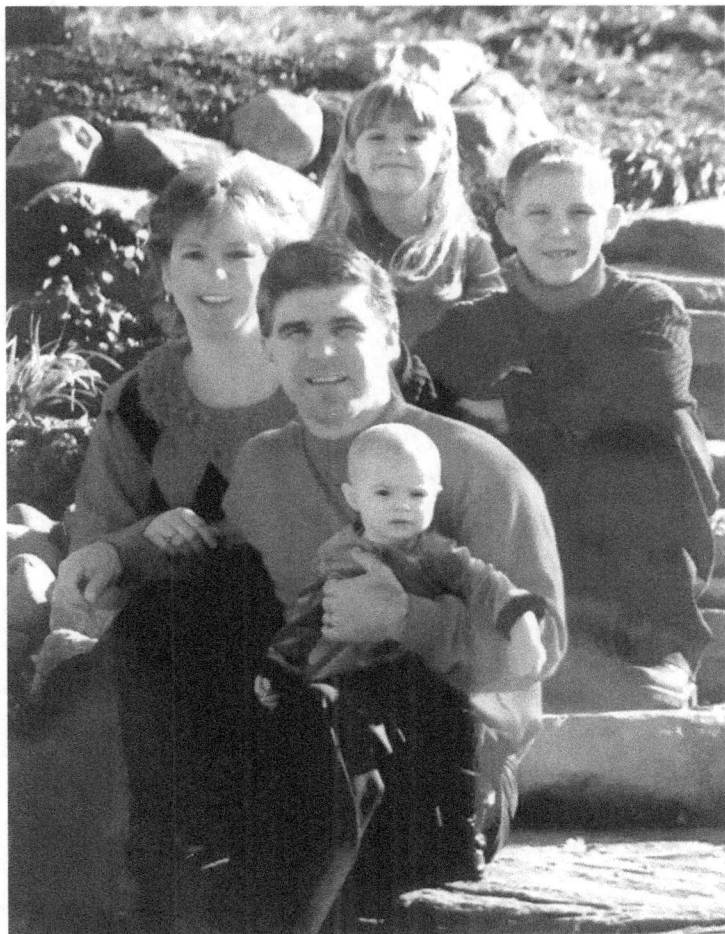

Stacy, Tim holding Kaleigh, McKala, and Kyle

WEEK EIGHT

Truly I tell you, if you have faith as small
as a mustard seed, you can say to this mountain,
"Move from here to there," and it will move.
Nothing will be impossible for you.
(Matthew 17:20)

GREEN BEAN FAITH!

One fall afternoon my wife, Stacy, had just completed fixing a nice dinner and our family had sat down to have our meal together. Those times are more frequent when the children are younger, as many activities seem to get in the way of families having dinner together these days.

My son had been acting up a little during dinner. We all have a food that rubs our taste palette in the wrong direction. This food for my son undoubtedly was green beans. From the time he was an infant, anything that looked like a green bean, smelled like a green bean, or tasted like a green bean was not going down his throat into his stomach. All parents practice their parenting skills through experimentations on their first-born child, and Stacy and I were no exception. Kyler had acted up at the dinner table and I knew he didn't like green beans, so I decided to be a little bit creative in my disciplinary measure. I would make him eat green beans.

After much pleading, begging, and salesmanship on his part, Kyler lost the battle, and Dad's word was firm: he must eat the green beans or pay the price. What was the price? I don't know. Stacy and I as young parents had not gotten that far. I must inform you that there were only two green beans on his plate. While we were still at the dinner table, we watched our son painfully roll his green beans from side to side in deep thought about how he was going to accomplish this awful task that his mean parents had mandated he perform.

We watched him take the first green bean, cut it up into little pieces, hold his nose, chew the green bean, and hold his head back as he forced himself to swallow it. Of course, after the first green bean was down he gagged as if it were coming back up.

At this point my wife and I excused ourselves from the table to take care of some tasks that needed done after dinner. While I was in the other room my mind began to think of wise older people in my life, using quotes like "The apple doesn't fall far from the tree," "Paybacks are a bummer," and my mother specifically saying that she hoped she lived long enough to see my children put her through what I put her through." (I really was a good kid for the most part.) I'm not sure where the love is in these statements, but for sure I knew my parents loved us kids.

As I was thinking of these quotes, I got this idea that my son was probably at the kitchen table sliding his last green bean underneath the table and feeding it to our dog, who would eat ten pounds of whatever food we put in front of her. So, I thought I would be the professional parent and tiptoe through the living room, sneak around the corner, and peak my head into the kitchen to catch my son doing this dirty deed.

What I was about to see was a life lesson I'll never forget. There sat my four-year-old son rolling the last green bean back and forth on his plate with his fork in what I assumed was deep thought about how he could make it disappear without his father catching him. He then abruptly laid his fork down on the table, folded his hands in a prayer-like position, and said in a boldness that only a child's voice can use, "Dear God, please help this green bean to turn into a noodle."

You guessed it--my heart melted. I was overwhelmed that my son's childlike faith considered God big enough to turn a green bean into a noodle. He no longer had to worry about eating the green bean because his dad was passed out on the floor laughing, and he could have given the green bean to the dog. I proceeded to cut the green bean in half and told my son that he had to eat only half of the green bean and that I would eat the other half.

The Bible speaks clearly about us coming to our daddy Father in Heaven with childlike faith. In our years of experience as we grow older, it seems that our childlike faith is easily dwindled. It's great for us to observe a little child living out his or her faith. It's my prayer as a dad that as my children grow older they will never leave that childlike faith they have in our great God.

PRINCIPLE FOR LIVING:
Choose to live with a big faith.

WEEK NINE

*God so loved the world that he gave
his one and only Son, that whoever believes in
him shall not perish but have eternal life.*
(John 3:16)

HOW GREAT IS A FATHER'S LOVE?

Most of the lessons learned in this book are the life lessons learned from my children Kyler, McKala, and Kaleigh; however, there are a few lessons that I have learned from our children who reside in heaven with their Heavenly Father as Stacy and I experienced four miscarriages.

This is one of those lessons. Have you ever seen something that made you instinctively turn your head because you couldn't bear the sight? I think of those I have worked with in my counseling office who have had to identify the bodies of their loved ones after fatal vehicle accidents. I think of those parents who could not bear to look when the handcuffs went on the wrists of their sons or daughters after being arrested for committing a crime. I think about mothers who turn their heads when they see their children in pain from an injury. I think about my own son, who was delivered prematurely and not breathing. It was pain so great that I could not bear the sight.

The Bible tells us that when Jesus, God's only begotten Son, was put through the most excruciating and gruesome pain that any human being has ever suffered to bear the sins of all humanity, God the Father could not bear to look. He turned His head.

I am reminded of the most popular verse in all of Scripture, John 3:16--"God so loved the world that he gave his one and only Son, that whoever believes in him shall not perish but have eternal life." The difference between us as humans turning our heads when seeing our painful situations and God the Father turning His head when His Son was being crucified is that God the Father *chose* for His Son to go through that severe pain so that you and I might endure and forge through the difficult pains of our lives in His strength and ultimately reside in heaven for all eternity, where there will be no more pain, no more tears, and no more sorrow.

Let me urge you: if you are in the midst of life's pain today, please run to the comforting presence of the Father's love.

PRINCIPLE FOR LIVING:

Nothing will ever separate you
from the love of God.

WEEK TEN

The peace of God, which transcends
all understanding, will guard your hearts
and your minds in Christ Jesus.
(Philippians 4:7)

WANT PEACEFUL SLEEP?

On Saturday March 13, 2004, my three-year-old daughter, Kaleigh, came over and crawled up into my lap to give me hugs and kisses. There is this standing competition in my household as to who gets all the "hugs and kisses" from Kaleigh.

While she sat on my lap and hugged on me in the middle of a Saturday afternoon after an incredibly busy week, I said to little Kaleigh, "Daddy is going to pray to Jesus." As we bowed our heads and I prayed and thanked my Heavenly Father for the blessing of this little three-year-old delight, I became more aware that all children are a gift from above. Kaleigh was truly a blessing in that my wife and I had tried many years to conceive and spent thousands of dollars at a fertility doctor.

The highlight of this story came when I said, "In Jesus's name. Amen." It was then that Kaleigh said, "Daddy, it's my turn." To listen to the innocence of a three-year-old go before the throne of grace is nothing less than overwhelming and awesome. To hear her thank Jesus that Mommy and Daddy tuck her in every night before bedtime and pray to Jesus is worth all the money in the entire world.

I wonder if the deep, peaceful sleep that she encounters every night has anything to do with Mommy and Daddy tucking her in, telling her that we love her, and bringing her before the Daddy of all daddies in prayer. We adults would be wise to humble ourselves and go before Abba Father (Galatians 4:6) and thank Him for His many blessings, praise Him for who He is-- and just maybe our sleep would include the peace that passes all human understanding (Philippians 4:7).

PRINCIPLE FOR LIVING:

Pray about every situation.

Give thanks in good times as well as bad times.

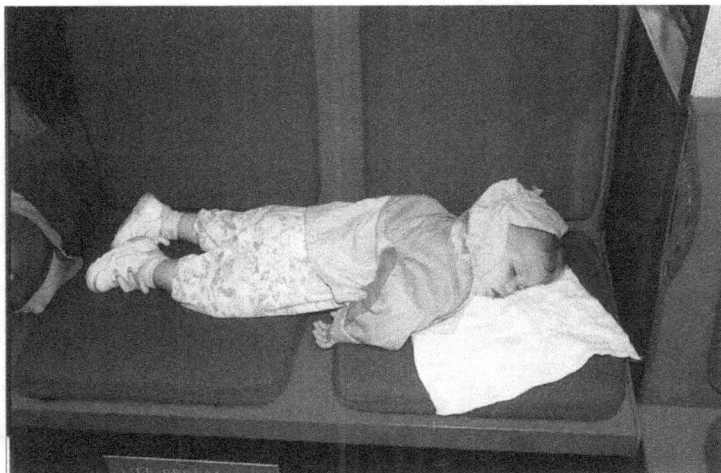

McKala sleeping on the boat to Mackinac Island

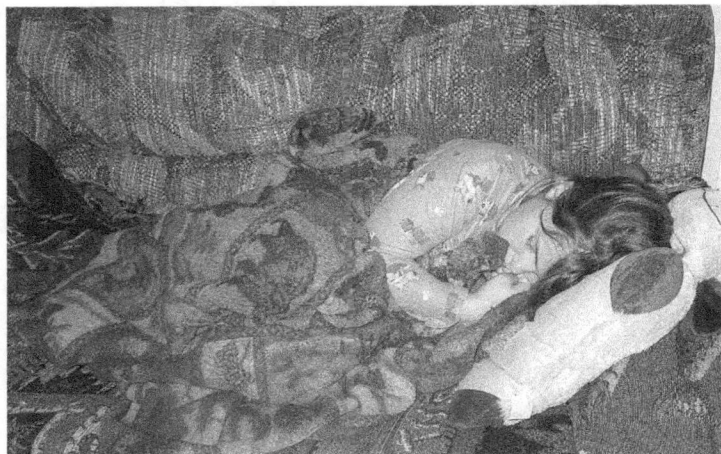

Kaleigh sleeping at the cabin

WEEK ELEVEN

Create in me a pure heart, O God,
and renew a steadfast spirit within me.
(Psalm 51:10)

A 180-DEGREE TURN

My wife and I are truly thankful for our three great kids. Our parenting career has not been without bumps in the road, however.

In July 2005 my only son had lied to his mother and me in regard to him and his two friends crashing our four-wheelers. We had disciplined our son for that incident with what I will call "a grounding on steroids," otherwise known as a "blackout" (a loss of all privileges).

My wife and I were lying in bed one evening discussing the subject of when we would know how and when to give back our son some of his privileges. We agreed that we needed to see repentance in his heart for what he had done.

About three weeks later the family was in church and the pastor was preaching a sermon from the Scriptures on the subject of David and Bathsheba. David had committed adultery with Bathsheba, which led to lies and even murder. When David finally came to his senses and repented to God, he said, "Against you, you only, have I sinned" (Psalm 51:4), acknowledging that his wrongs were directed toward God the Father.

While in church that Sunday morning, I remember vividly my son sitting at the end of the row. Beside him sat his sister, then his mother, then me. It did not surprise me that he sat as far away from his father as he could. I am sure he may have sat on the other side of the auditorium with some friends had we permitted him to do so.

As our pastor began to talk about the subject of repentance, I noticed that my son began to well up with tears. This was my first sign that my son had understood his wrongs and had begun repentance. Later that evening my wife and I had made our way over to some friends' house. My son had remained home fulfilling a list of chores he had been given. I received a phone call from him, and there was an urgency in his voice as he said, "Dad, I need to talk to you right away."

I told him to drive over to our friends' house. I met him in the back of their house, and he and I began to walk down the driveway. My son broke down in uncontrollable tears and said to me, "Dad it doesn't matter to me if I'm grounded the rest of my life--I just need to know you and Mom forgive me for what I did." It was then that I knew with tears flowing down my cheeks as well that my son understood the message of repentance. My wife and I knew we could safely begin giving back some of his privileges.

Ironically, or according to the sovereignty of God, I left my home the next morning for my nine o'clock appointment with a young man I had been working with since he was fourteen. When I initially met his mother, she was dressed in unkempt and inappropriate attire. This young man had wept in my office many times trying to explain in his own words his longing for a relationship with his father, who was in prison.

This young man is one of the politest with whom I've ever worked. He has a great sense of humor and loves the game of baseball, which is one of many connections we have. There is a world full of fatherless young men who need the bond of a father figure who lives out and exemplifies the love that exists between God the Father and God the Son. What God has taught me through the incident with my son is that this type of love can be exhibited only when true repentance has taken place.

PRINCIPLE FOR LIVING:

Model a repentant spirit to your children and
look for a repentant spirit in them
after they are disciplined.

Kyler at Lake Center Christian School

WEEK TWELVE

How long will you lie there, you sluggard?
When will you get up from your sleep? A little sleep,
a little slumber, a little folding of the hands to rest--
and poverty will come on you like a thief
and scarcity like an armed man.
(Proverbs 6:9-11)

DON'T LET THE BIG ONE GET AWAY!

While there are many research studies that determine how much sleep we need, the Scriptures caution us to not sleep too much. Too much sleep (laziness) can lead to poverty.

You will learn throughout this book that our family loves to be outdoors. There were many times that my children and I would get up before daylight and head out into a hunting blind or a double tree stand to enjoy the great outdoors and hope that a big white-tail buck would wonder close to us. There were many times I would look over at my children after daylight only to find that they were fast asleep. On one occasion my son, Kyler, was up a tree approximately five yards away from me, and I noticed his head leaning forward with his forehead on a cushioned front rail. He was fast asleep.

As luck would have it, I noticed a nice eight-point buck headed straight toward us. I did everything short of shouting (and thus alerting the deer) to wake Kyler up. I even threw pieces of candy at him only to have it fall to the ground while he remained asleep. The white-tail buck actually walked right under his tree stand.

Once I realized that he was not going to wake up, I drew my gun and pulled the trigger. After the incredibly loud bang and watching the whitetail buck run about eighty yards, I looked over at Kyler, and--believe it or not--he had not budged. The deep sleep that I'm sure his little body needed cost him his first harvest in the whitetail hunting world.

I have found that if you have a God-sized goal, you will rest your body to regain energy but eagerly get out of bed in the morning to tackle that God-sized goal He has placed on your heart. A little sleep, a little slumber– and the "big one" will get away.

PRINCIPLE FOR LIVING:

God honors hard work in the
balance of right priorities.

Tim and Kyler hunting

WEEK THIRTEEN

*Nothing in all creation is hidden from God's sight.
Everything is uncovered and laid bare before the eyes of
him to whom we must give account.*

(Hebrews 4:13)

GOD SEES ALL

Most of the life lessons learned in this book are from stories when my children were at a young age. However, there are a few from when my children were older. One of those came when Stacy, our girls, and I traveled to Florida to watch Kyler play college baseball his freshman year. He attended Cedarville (Ohio) University, a Division 2 university, and they had opened up their season in Florida, as it is way too cold for baseball in Ohio during that time of the year. Being part of a liberal arts Christian university, the team attended church services on Sunday morning prior to their games beginning on Monday.

When we arrived at the church and attempted to find a seat in the multi-thousand-seat auditorium, we knew that the probability of seeing the team was slim to none. We wandered up into the balcony and found four empty seats in the front row on the far-left side. The message from the pastor that day was on parenting. He stated that all parents make their firstborn guinea pigs as they learn to parent.

He then asked if there were any guinea pigs in the audience. It was then that I noticed that the Cedarville baseball team was seated right below us on the first level, and my son, Kyler, was raising both hands, making it clear that his parents had practiced on him, making him a guinea pig as well. I immediately got my phone out and texted him, "This is God, and I just saw you raise both your hands!"

As his phone vibrated in his pocket, he pulled it out and read it. He slowly turned his head and looked up behind him at the sly expression on my face and my waving hand. He looked in disbelief and shook his head. Most college freshmen look forward to having some independence away from their parents. I'm sure he thought, "I'm twenty-one hours away from home, and my mom and dad are still watching over me!" Had I known what "LOL" stood for at that time, I would have texted it to him.

The Bible tells us that the eyes of God are everywhere and that He sees our every move. Stacy and I taught our children a little song with lyrics that go something like this: "Oh, be careful, little eyes, what you see. . .. Oh, be careful, little ears, what you hear. . .. Oh, be careful, little feet, where you go. . .. For the Father up above, He is looking down with love. Oh, be careful . . ." Sobering words, aren't they? Truly understanding the omniscience of God changes the way we live. What does God see that you need to start working on changing today?

PRINCIPLE FOR LIVING:

Character is living life fully knowing that
God sees all we do.

WEEK FOURTEEN

Rejoice in the Lord always. I will say it again: Rejoice!
(Philippians 4:4)

ARE YOU HAVING A GOOD DAY?

It was a warm, beautiful spring day, and I was watching my four-year-old daughter, McKala, while my wife, Stacy, went to pick up our son, Kyler. We were sitting down to have some lunch and I asked McKala to say a prayer and thank Jesus for the food we were going to eat. Of course, I could lead in prayer as I had many times before, but given my druthers, I would much rather hear my children pray their childlike faith prayers.

McKala began to pray, "Dear Jesus, thank You for this beautiful, wonderful day." The interesting note in the opening line of her prayer was that our food got cold while she was saying the words *beautiful* and *wonderful*. She dragged out the syllables forever. Talk about making a point! She wanted God to know that the day was beautiful and wonderful.

After she said, "Amen," and we began eating our lunch, as had happened many times before, my young child sent me into a whirlwind of deep thoughts. I began especially after lunch to ponder her dragging out the syllables of those two words. The Scriptures came to mind that we are to rejoice always, for this is the day the Lord has made. Not only does God choose to give us days here on earth, but if we really put things into perspective, most days are indeed beautiful and wonderful. I think the Apostle Paul would even label his days as beautiful and wonderful while he was sitting in prison when he said he counted it all joy.

When you and I stop and ponder all our blessings, this truly *is* a beautiful and wonderful day. As I write this short story, it is cloudy, gray, cold, and snowing outside--but due to the Sonshine in the hearts of McKala and her dad, this truly is a *beautiful* and *wonderful* day.

PRINCIPLE FOR LIVING:

Every day can be a good day when
our focus is on eternity.

WEEK FIFTEEN

Our struggle is not against flesh and blood,
but against the rulers, against the authorities, against
the powers of this dark world and against the spiritual
forces of evil in the heavenly realms.

(Ephesians 6:12)

DEATH IS SURE

One of the most difficult losses anyone can ever experience is the loss of a child. Grief experts say that the deepest, darkest hours of grief are in the loss of a child. I watched my mom grieve the loss of my sister Marsha firsthand.

Stacy and I are blessed with three incredible children, who inspired me to write this book. I would be remiss not to mention the four children we lost during pregnancy. We don't always understand the plans of God, but we trust in His sovereignty, and losing four children makes us all the more thankful for the three children God has allowed us to raise.

One day when Kyler was around seven years of age, I was driving down the road when out of the clear blue he said, "Dad, I know why Baby King died." This was soon after Stacy and I lost a baby during her fifth month of pregnancy. It was the toughest miscarriage, at least for me, as we had to file a death certificate and Stacy had to have surgery right after the loss.

I was all ears when Kyler made this profound statement. I asked him, "Why did Baby King die?"

His answer was immediate and matter-of-fact. He said, "Baby King died because of the devil." Kyler went on to explain that the devil is ultimately behind all bad things.

Kyler was right. Death and the grief we feel when losing a loved one originated as a result of sin. It would be easy to blame Adam and Eve, and yet I personally have sinned multiple times--and Adam and Eve did not make me do it. Kyler gave us an understanding to that age-old question "Why do bad things happen to good people?"

I can remember the day after the conversation with young Kyler, determining to direct any ill-will feelings that I had toward the father of death, namely the devil. I can remember determining to serve in a greater way the Giver of all life, namely God. I am grateful to God for teaching me this profound lesson through my seven-year-old.

PRINCIPLE FOR LIVING:

Live today as if it would be your last--
as someday it will.

WEEK SIXTEEN

*Teach them to your children, talking about
them when you sit at home and when you walk along
the road, when you lie down and when you get up.*
(Deuteronomy 11:19)

WHAT KIND OF MAN IS THIS?

You will find mentioned throughout this book that our family has grown to thoroughly enjoy the great outdoors. Scripture tells us to look for ways to talk with our children and other people about the precepts of God (Deuteronomy 11:19). I have often said that the best life lived is a life lived on principled truths. We cannot choose to live by principled truth if we are unaware of them.

On one beautiful summer day my daughter McKala and I had the privilege of going fishing off the New Jersey shore with some good friends of ours. McKala quickly found out that a thirty-five-foot fishing boat out on the ocean on a windy day was anything but calm. It was rather comical watching her attempt to balance herself while standing and moving from one point to the next in the boat.

It was then that I seized the opportunity to remind her of the story in the Scriptures where Jesus calmed a tremendous storm on the water. The story is found in the fourth chapter of Mark. When the men in the boat saw Jesus remaining calm in the midst of a severe storm that could ultimately take their lives, they asked a question: "What manner of man is this, that the winds and the waves obey his command?" What a great opportunity to teach my daughter to always put her trust in Jesus when in the midst of life storms! We talked about Jesus having no surprises in His world. We also talked about the sovereign attribute of God. Let me ask you a question.

Where do you turn when the circumstances of life put you in the midst of a storm? As a professional counselor, I have seen people turn to all kinds of unstable things when they find themselves in the midst of life's storms. I have seen them turn to alcohol, drugs, dysfunctional relationships, and even professional counseling.

I hope the lesson taught to my daughter that day on the boat reminds her to turn to trust the only One who can give us peace that passes all human under-standing (Philippians 4:7) and calm the storms in our life.

PRINCIPLE FOR LIVING:

When in the middle of life's trials,
always turn to Jesus first.

Tim and Kaleigh fishing at OBX

Kyler, Tim, and McKala fishing

WEEK SEVENTEEN

Every animal of the forest is mine,
and the cattle on a thousand hills.
(Psalm 50:10)

YOUR FATHER OWNS IT ALL

Have you ever stopped to ponder the busy-ness of life? According to a well-known say-ing, "Even if you reach the top of the corporate ladder--you'll find out that the ladder is leaning on the wrong wall." And don't forget the saying "If you win the rat race, you'll still be a rat!"

There are many good parents who fall prey to seek-ing security and significance through accumulating stuff. When will we learn that there will are no hearses pulling U-Hauls? It is indeed true that we cannot take anything with us to heaven other than the Holy Scriptures and the souls of humanity. I was reminded of these truths one summer day right after McKala had turned five years old. My wife and I were discussing our bills and budget at a time when money was pretty tight in our family. In an almost apologetic voice McKala said, "Hey, Dad, if I had prayed for you since I was four years old, you would be rich by now."

Right then and there it dawned on me: that's exactly why my wife and I were having financial difficulty, because my children had failed to pray for their daddy to become rich! No, I'm just kidding. But in all seriousness, my daughter believed that her Heavenly Father was rich and He is the giver of all good things (James 1:17).

Do you believe that? The truth of the matter is this--that whatever we have, it all belongs to Him. There is nothing wrong with financial gain even to the point of being considered wealthy. But make no mistake: whether you have little or you have much, it all belongs to God the Father. Money, and most of the time the lack thereof, is the number-one thing couples fight about. I have personally seen this issue destroy marriages.

What would change in your life if you begin praying about how to manage the income God gives you? What would happen to those of you who are without work if you began praying to the Father in heaven, who owns it all, to help you find employment? Who knows? Maybe if you began praying now, you might just be rich one year from now. Maybe not monetarily, but inevitably you will be rich as your relationship with your Creator will become more intimate as you talk to Him.

PRINCIPLE FOR LIVING:

Everything you have belongs to God.

WEEK EIGHTEEN

Carry each other's burdens, and in this way,
you will fulfill the law of Christ.
(Galatians 6:2)

GOD'S LANGUAGE OF LOVE

When my wife and I got married I explained to her how I wanted to have five boys so that I could have my own in-house basketball team. You guessed it, ladies: my wife was not on board with that program. She explained that she wanted only three children. Well, there was an easy compromise for my wife and me: we set out to have four children.

We may have made our own plans, but the Word of God tells us that God's plans trump our plans (Proverbs

16:9). I tell people that I ended up with a point guard and two cheerleaders. Actually, my daughters played sports as well, and neither of them were cheerleaders. *My wife believed in natural childbirth, and she did it three times with our children.*

I have said to my wife, Stacy, that we're even now, since I've also "given birth" three times--to those incredibly painful things called kidney stones. One of the first questions I'll ask my Heavenly Father when I get to heaven is "What was the purpose of kidney stones?"

Well, sometimes God gives us a little glimpse of His purposes here on earth, and I received one of those little glimpses when I came home from the hospital after my kidney stone surgery. I was lying on the couch, and to be honest, I'm not really sure how much medication Stacy had tricked me into taking. I do remember this powerful truth that came from my daughter McKala. While I was lying on the couch recovering from surgery, my daughter began to cry. I asked her, "Why are you crying? It's not *your* body that's hurting."

Now I know that might not be the greatest stint of being a father in my parenting career, but nevertheless it's how the story went down. In her innocent little voice McKala began to explain to me that even though it wasn't her body and her own boo-boos, she loved me--and that's why she was crying. The Scripture verse that came to my mind was "Carry each other's burdens, and in this way, you will fulfill the law of Christ" (Galatians 6:2).

When we see a relative, a friend, or a brother or sister in Christ hurting, we are told by Jesus, who exemplified true compassion and love, to bear their burdens with them. When our life here on earth comes to an end, all that will ultimately matter will be relationships we have built. Going through others' difficult circumstances with them deepens relationships. Think about people you know right now who are going through difficult times. Please take the time to reach out to them and bear their burdens, because after all, Jesus is the one who understands best the language of my daughter's tears.

Principle for Living:
Encourage others who are living in the
midst of a burden.

WEEK NINETEEN

(Mother's Day)

Her children arise and call her blessed;
her husband also, and he praises her.
(Proverbs 31:28)

THE DYNAMIC OF A MOTHER'S LOVE

My biological father passed away when I was just two-and-a-half years old. An incredible loving mother raised me for almost a decade in a single-parent home. As I have experienced and watched the dynamic of a mother's love in action, I have continually been astonished by its power. Proverbs 31 speaks about this type of mother.

All three of our children were very fond of the golden retriever dogs we have had in our home since the inception of our family. One of those we named Attie, which was short for attitude. She was a reminder for our children to choose to have a good attitude. The mother of my three children decided to have our golden retriever bred. The result was eleven tiny, cuddly, cute, and lovable puppies. (Did I just say that?) Why do I feel like I should turn in my man card?

Stacy was able to teach our children many lessons as they watched the mother of these eleven little puppies feed them, protect them, and meet their need for safety and security. The following is what McKala, then in the fifth grade, wrote about her mother in a Mother's Day card.

> *Dear Mom,*
>
> *I know a mom who wishes she could have a day off, go shopping all she wants, and do no chores. She has no day off, can't go shopping all she wants, and has to do chores instead. I know a mom who is very nice and loving and caring and hardly ever yells or is mean. I know a mom who gives kisses and hugs to her family. We give her kisses and hugs in return. I know a mom who loves taking care of her family and go-*

ing shopping and believes she can do anything with Christ's help. This mom is very special, and I'm thankful and very glad this special mother is mine!

These kinds of lessons are priceless.

Principle for Living:
Honor the position God has given
your mother today.

Kyler, Stacy holding Kaleigh, and McKala

WEEK TWENTY

*We have seen and testify that the Father has sent
his Son to be the Savior of the world.*
(1 John 4:14)

TREE HOUSE CARPENTER

When Stacy and I first got married we lived in a small 800-square-foot duplex. We graduated up to an approximately 1,000-square-foot duplex just before Kyler, our first child, was born. Right outside of our duplex on our property was a group of trees that I noticed would be perfect for a tree house. Out came the hammer and saw. It became one of those projects that was more exciting for Dad than it was for his son. I could envision what the tree house would look like after the finished product was completed, but his little mind could not. Of course, my purpose was to create a tree house for Kyler and his friends to get away to, be adventurous, and just play as little boys do.

God always has a bigger, better, and most of the time different plan. Kyler's mom is five feet two inches tall and I myself am five feet eight inches tall, which meant that our children were most likely not going to be giants in the land.

One day while climbing the rope ladder to get into the tree house with my son, Kyler, I thought of the story in the Bible in which Zacchaeus had climbed a sycamore tree to get Jesus's attention. I remember sitting on the floor of this four-by-six-foot tree house with my son and telling him how important it was to this man named Zacchaeus to get a glimpse of Jesus (Luke 19). I likened it to the desire to shake the hand of a famous athlete like Michael Jordan or LeBron James, since my son was playing YMCA basketball at the time. I attempted in my own feeble way to explain how much more important and how much bigger the man Jesus Christ was than these famous athletes.

I explained to him that it was trees that made the

cross on which Jesus would be crucified. I explained to him that during Jesus's years on earth, of all the professions he could have chosen, he chose to be a carpenter. The most important thing I explained to Kyler in the tree house was that what He did as a carpenter was not the most important thing that he did on earth. You see, Jesus was more than a carpenter. I explained to Kyler that Jesus came to this earth to be our Savior, to reach out to needy people like Zacchaeus and like him and me. He came to earth to reach out to people like you as well.

As I write this story, I'm so proud to tell you that Kyler is no longer seven years old. He is a young man and continues to serve Christ, to worship Him, to talk to Him, and to the best of his ability to follow Him. There are many days I wish I still had that tree house to remind me of these vital life lessons that I pray we will never forget.

PRINCIPLE FOR LIVING:

Jesus was more than a carpenter.
He is the Savior of humanity.

The Kings with friends in the treehouse

WEEK TWENTY-ONE

(Memorial Day)

*No one will be able to stand against you
all the days of your life. As I was with Moses, so I will be
with you; I will never leave you nor forsake you.*

(Joshua 1:5)

NEVER ALONE!

While riding in my "midlife crisis car," a convertible Mustang, with my six-year-old daughter, Kaleigh, I was trying to count in my head how many people were going out to eat with us. We were going out with our good friends, the Martins. As I was counting Kaleigh interrupted me by saying, "Dad, there are not two of us in this car--there are four of us in this car because God and Jesus are with us wherever we go." She then proceeded to mention Grandma

Hamilton and our golden retriever dog, both of whom had gone to heaven, being with us as well.

Matthew 18:20 tells us that where two or three people are gathered in the name of Christ Jesus, He is there as well. Joshua 1:5 reminds us that He promises never to leave us or forsake us. My heart was touched by Kaleigh's words of wisdom, but then the conversation quickly digressed when she told me that she had a boyfriend! I proceeded to give Kaleigh five expositional reasons as to why she would not have a boyfriend until she was thirty years old.

Principle for Living:

Once you have given your life to Jesus,
He will never abandon you.

WEEK TWENTY-TWO

All the earth bows down to you;
they sing praise to you, they sing the praises of your
name (Psalm 66:4). Let them praise the name of the LORD,
for his name alone is exalted; his splendor is above the
earth and the heavens. And he has raised up for his
people a horn, the praise of all his faithful servants, of
Israel, the people close to his heart. Praise the LORD.
(Psalm 148:13-14)

BASEBALL IN HEAVEN

I t was just another beautiful late spring day
when my son, Kyler, and I loaded the car once
again to head out to one of his baseball games. I must
admit that some of the most exciting times in Stacy's

and my parenting career was heading off to watch our children compete in athletic events. My wife and I both participated in sports growing up, and all three of our children did as well.

On this particular trip to a baseball game, Kyler with his inquisitive mind looked over at me as I was driving and asked, "Dad, is there baseball in heaven?" I proceeded to give my son the best of my humor and told him that I believe so and that God's favorite sport is baseball. Kyler then looked at me with excitement in his voice and said, "Baseball is God's favorite sport?"

I replied, "Yes, the Bible says at the beginning of the Bible, "In the 'big inning' God created the heavens and the earth." (I must admit that a joke is not nearly as funny if you have to explain it as I did to my young son.

I then asked Kyler why he had asked the question. His response was enlightening to say the least. There is this common cheer that a team does when some-one does well. It goes something like this: "Let's go, Kyler--let's go!" The cheer is then repeated over and over again. Kyler began to explain that if indeed base-ball was in heaven that everybody would be cheering, "Let's go, Jesus--let's go!" over and over again.

What a profound insight my little son gave me! The Bible says in Psalms that all earth and heaven proclaim His name. The Psalms are full of praises that echo out the name of Jesus. I do believe that Kyler's statement was true. Someday we will all step on the shores of heaven, and our first desire will be to see the face of Jesus. The Bible tells us we will praise His name throughout all eternity.

Maybe we should begin to do as my son taught me that day--to praise His name today and every day. Maybe your family is not doing so well, or maybe you're not doing so well yourself. Maybe your "team" at work or at your church is not doing so well. Why not begin a chant? "Let's go, Jesus--let's go!"

Principle for Living:

Jesus is your biggest fan.

Let's praise Him today and every day.

Kyler ready to throw a pitch

WEEK TWENTY-THREE

(Father's Day)

Then Jesus came to them and said,
"All authority in heaven and on earth has been
given to me. Therefore go and make disciples of all na-
tions, baptizing them in the name of the Father
and of the Son and of the Holy Spirit."
(Matthew 28:18-19)

A GOD-SIZED GOAL FOR ANY DAD

Some of my most precious keepsakes are hanging in my office bathroom. They are birthday cards, Father's Day cards, and "just-because" cards from my kids. Most of them are homemade. If my office building were on fire, I would run straight to my bathroom to collect these irreplaceable keepsakes. Ka-

leigh Rae, my youngest child who has the same middle
name as her father, wrote this to me on the Father's
Day when she was eight years old:

> *I love you so much. You are the best dad ever.*
> *I hope you really like my present. Thank you*
> *for everything you do for us. Grandma [my late*
> *mother] is proud of you and so is God becuz [be-*
> *cause] you always help others and show people*
> *Christ. Happy Father's Day, Dad. You really are a*
> *wonderful speishal [special] creashion [creation]*
> *of God. Your hart [heart] is so big. I love you, Dad.*
>
> *Sinserally [Sincerely],*
> *Kaleigh*

Here is the God-sized goal for any father. It is to
have your children grow up to call you their hero. If
I can develop an intimate and loving relationship with
my children, always help others, show people Christ,
and make God proud of me, there is a good chance
I will accomplish this goal. How do you want your children to remember you?

PRINCIPLE FOR LIVING:

Love God and love people. That's it, and that's all.

Tim's office door with handmade cards from the kids and nephews

WEEK TWENTY-FOUR

If you declare with your mouth, "Jesus is Lord,"
and believe in your heart that God raised him from
the dead, you will be saved.
(Romans 10:9)

A PARENT'S GREATEST MOMENT

I often say that there are two very important questions every individual should ask himself or herself. The first and most important is one with eternal ramifications: "If I were to die today, do I know for sure that I would spend eternity in heaven?" The next two most important questions a person can be asked in my opinion has to do with his or her identity: "Who am I?" and "Who am I becoming?" This short story focuses on the first question.

I can't begin to count the number of days that I have driven my children to athletic practices and/or games. One baseball practice I drove my son to is etched in my mind forever. Kyler loaded up his bat bag and got dressed for his baseball practice, and he and I put on our matching ball caps, as I was one of his coaches. We then headed off to the practice field.

On the previous Sunday Kyler had learned in church about the Christmas and Easter stories. He had learned that God had created him as well as the entire universe. He had learned that God had sent his only Son, Jesus, born to a virgin named Mary. He learned that Jesus lived on earth thirty-three years and then died a cruel death on a cross. He learned that Jesus rose from His grave on the third day and that He currently resides in heaven.

Kyler with his young eight-year-old mind was asking some pretty inquisitive questions for his age. On our way to practice he boldly said that he wanted to pray a prayer and receive God's gift, Jesus, into his life so that his sins would be forgiven and he would spend eternity forever in heaven someday.

All of a sudden how good he was in baseball seemed to fade into the distance. Our win-loss record became miniscule. What kind of equipment and how expensive the equipment was becoming minor. This was not just any little boy--this was my son desiring the greatest gift that has ever been given to humanity: a personal relationship with his Creator and the promise of eternity in heaven.

I know it shouldn't seem so simple, and yet it is. Romans 10:9 says that if we believe in our heart and confess with our mouth that God has raised His Son from the dead (the Easter story), then we will have eternal life in heaven with God.

It didn't take me long to determine that being late to practice that day was okay. I promptly pulled our van over off the side of the road, and Kyler and I prayed together. To hear my eight-year-old son pray a simple prayer and ask Jesus into his heart and ask him to forgive him of the wrong things he had done is absolutely and unexplainably priceless.

Kyler and I embraced each other and thanked God for His gift, and yes, it was allergy season here in

Ohio. Showing up to baseball practice with a little water in our eyes looked as if we had just had an allergy attack. At least that's what the big boys tell their big-boy friends!

I encourage all parents who read this story to make it an absolute top priority to make sure your children know and have a personal relationship with Jesus Christ. I have seen my children accomplish many things in their short lives. I have seen them selected as the most valuable player, I have seen them elected to the all-county team, I have seen them be the all-star and high scorer of the game, I have seen them hit homeruns, I have seen them get straight A's on their report cards, I have seen them get lead roles in plays-- and I promise you that none of them compares to that day. It truly is the greatest moment in a parent's life to see his or her children come to faith in Christ Jesus.

PRINCIPLE FOR LIVING:

A deep, intimate relationship with your
Creator is yours for the asking.

Kyler hitting the baseball

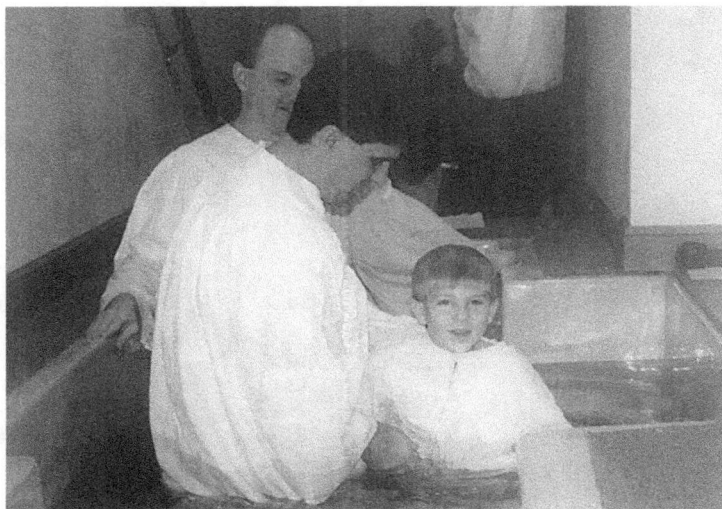

Tim baptizing Kyler

WEEK TWENTY-FIVE

(July 4)

*Once you were alienated from God and were
enemies in your minds because of your evil behavior.
But now he has reconciled you by Christ's physical
body through death to present you holy in his sight,
without blemish and free from accusation.*
(Colossians 1:21-22)

*There is now no condemnation for those
who are in Christ Jesus, because through
Christ Jesus the law of the Spirit who gives life has
set you free from the law of sin and death. For what the
law was powerless to do because it was weakened by the
flesh, God did by sending his own Son in the likeness of
sinful flesh to be a sin offering. And so, he condemned sin
in the flesh, in order that the righteous requirement of*

the law might be fully met in us, who do not live accord-

ing to the flesh but according to the Spirit.

(Romans 8:1-4)

A BOLD, PATRIOTIC SIXTH-GRADER

One of the things I have definitely modeled and taught all three of my children is the importance of showing respect to the men and women, past and present, who have given their time in service to protect the freedoms our country bestows upon us.

None of us will ever forget the tragedy of September 11, 2001. Unbeknownst to me, on the first-year anniversary of the tragedy, my son, Kyler, had asked his sixth-grade teacher if he would be permitted to lead his class in prayer and the Pledge of Allegiance to the United States flag as the president of our country had requested that schools and businesses pause at the noon hour in remembrance of September 11. As a dad I am prouder of moments like that than any of the times my son had made a great play on the athletic field or court. September 11 is certainly a time in history when we as parents can teach our children that freedom is not free.

There have been many times my children have held the hand of their mother and me as we prayed at the gravestone of my dad, who served our country in World War II. My children have been taught to stand at attention with utter reverence of the red, white, and blue flag that men and women have given their life to protect.

In the same vein, we have taught our children that spiritual freedom is not free either. We have taught them that it cost God the Father the price of willingly giving His only begotten Son to a cruel death upon a cross.

Are you grateful for the freedoms that are available to you as a result of the men and women who have given their lives and limbs for our country? Are you grateful to God the Father and Jesus, His Son, who willingly sacrificed that you and I might have spiritual freedom and eternal life in heaven when we pass from this life into the next? If you answer yes, please show that gratitude.

PRINCIPLE FOR LIVING:

Thank a veteran for his or her service and thank God on a regular basis for the blessing of spiritual freedom.

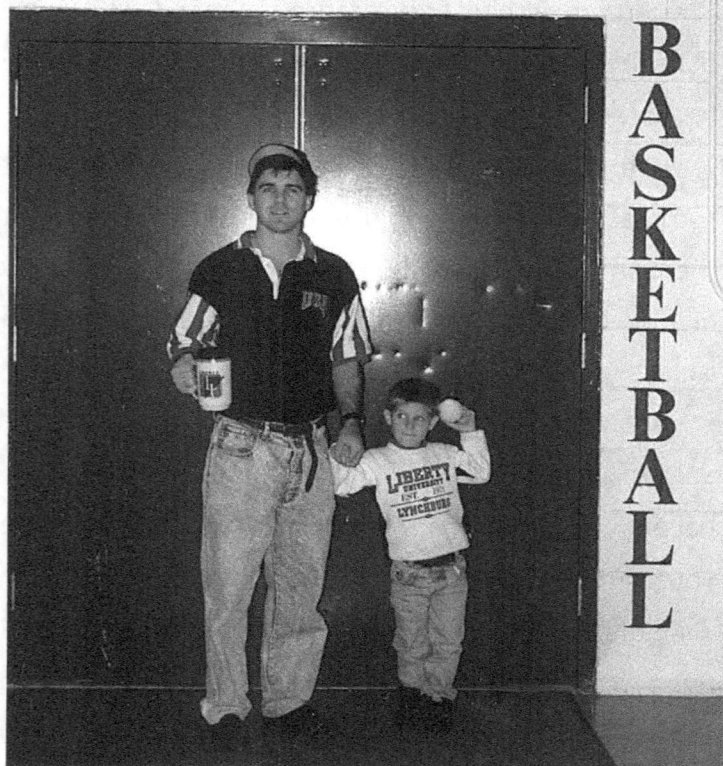

Tim and Kyler in red, white, and blue at a ball game

WEEK TWENTY-SIX

You created my inmost being; you knit me together
in my mother's womb. I praise you because
I am fearfully and wonderfully made; your works
are wonderful, I know that full well.
(Psalm 139:13-14)

THUMBODY SPECIAL

There's no greater news outside of the gospel message of Jesus Christ than the news that a husband and wife are expecting their firstborn. In October 1990 that news came to Stacy and me. I had heard that when a baby is born the baby is able to recognize the voice of his or her mother. Being the competitive spirit that I am, I wanted my newborn son to recognize his dad's voice as well.

Mom had a home court advantage, you might say. To even the playing field, I made it a point to attempt to sing my son lullabies before my wife and I would retire for the evening. These special solos for him usually came after my wife would say something in excitement like "Quick, quick--feel this kick!" or "Feel this, he is--he's rolling over!" The movement in my wife's belly was an indication that my son was awake and growing in the womb.

While he was awake I thought I would capture his attention with my stunning voice. Not! Keep in mind that the goal was not to woo him with my vibrato but simply to assure that he would recognize my voice on the day of his birth.

It began on July 11, 1991, at 2:00 in the morning when my wife shared with me those very unfamiliar words for the first time: "Daddy, my water just broke." It wasn't long afterward that we were on our way to the hospital for the birth of our very first child. Kyler came into the world exercising his vocal chords like a champion. I think the whole hospital heard him crying at the top of his lungs. I suppose it makes sense that when you are in a warm, safe place that one would cry upon leaving that environment, especially with the noises and bright lights that are so abundant in hospitals.

Kyler was about ten minutes old when one of the nurses brought him over to me while he was still screaming and said to me, "Dad, would you like to hold your new son?" That is like asking someone who has been in the desert for a week without water if he or she would like a drink of water.

"Of course, I would like to hold him," I said as I snatched my son from her arms so quickly that she probably thought I was a professional pickpocket in my day job.

This is where the story gets really interesting. As my son continued to scream at the top of his lungs, making his special debut into the world, I began to sing him one of those songs that I sang many times while he was still in his mother's tummy. As I stared at all eight pounds and fourteen ounces of him and his blue beanie cap, I began singing to him these words: "God made you thumbody special, thumbody special--God made you." It was like someone had turned off the switch. He instantaneously, after hearing me singing, stopped his crying and began looking back at me as though he recognized something.

Even the doctor and the nurses were wowed. One of the nurses commented, "He obviously knows your

voice." With this story comes two lessons: Lesson 1--
Are you listening to the still, small voice of your Creator? He is speaking and saying to you that He loves
you and created you on purpose for a purpose. Lesson
2--I have been telling my son most of his life that he
truly is a special creation of God. It is with this identity
that I want him to grow and live. It is with this identity that I pray he makes his decisions in life. It is with
this identity that I want all three of my children--Kyler,
McKala, and Kaleigh--to live their entire lives.

PRINCIPLE FOR LIVING:

God created you on purpose for a purpose.

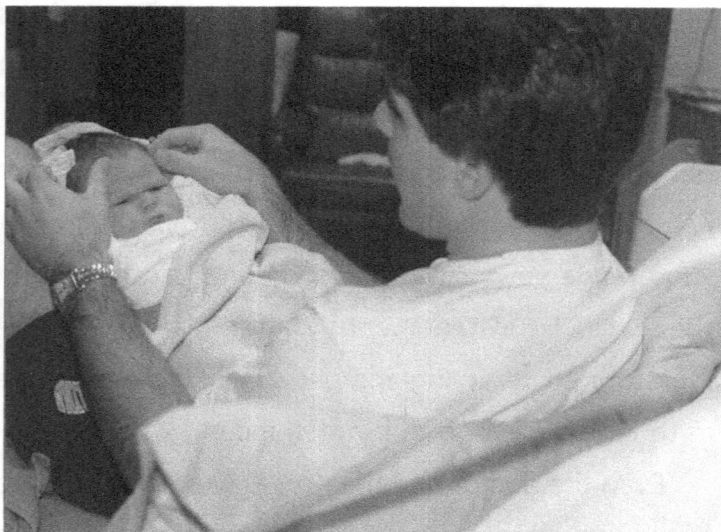

Tim holding Kyler

Tim and Kyler on the four-wheeler

WEEK TWENTY-SEVEN

Were I to count them [God's thoughts of me],
they would outnumber the grains of sand--when
I awake, I am still with you.
(Psalm 139:18)

Even the very hairs of your head are all numbered.
(Matthew 10:30)

GOD DOESN'T PLAY FAVORITES

I have been privileged to speak to audiences here in Ohio as well as in other states and countries. One summer I was invited to speak to students in the Atlanta area. It was a Christian church camp, where numerous churches came together for a week of fun and learning about God.

A young high schooler by the name of Tommy had decided to give his life to Jesus. Kyler, at the age of six, had traveled with me to this speaking engagement. While he and I were flying back from Atlanta, we began talking about the highlights of the camp experience. Kyler said, "Dad, I know who was your favorite kid at camp."

Since I had met hundreds of kids and have had some great times with many of them, my mind did not immediately go to Tommy. I responded to Kyler, "Oh, yeah? And who might this kid be?"

Kyler responded that it would be Tommy, who had given his life to Jesus. I began explaining to Kyler how I did like my new little brother in Christ, however; he was not my favorite kid at camp. Obviously, my son was thinking about all the kids he had met. I, though, was thinking about Kyler. I then told him that my favorite kid at camp was *by far* my favorite kid at camp and that this kid will be my favorite kid at *every* camp I speak at--when he is there.

His little mind finally caught on, and he exclaimed that *he* was my favorite kid! I seized the opportunity to explain that God does not pick favorites and that all who are His children are His favorite kids. I shared that the Bible points out that God says more good things about us than there are grains of sand on the beach and that He even knows how many hairs are on our head. It was yet another opportunity for me to tell my son that he is an incredible, special, creation of God.

PRINCIPLE FOR LIVING:

When Jesus was on the Cross, you were on His mind. You are His favorite!

WEEK TWENTY-EIGHT

*In everything I did, I showed you that by this
kind of hard work we must help the weak,
remembering the words the Lord Jesus himself said:
"It is more blessed to give than to receive".*
(Acts 20:35)

FATE, LUCK, COINCIDENCE,
OR A POWERFUL GOD?

This is a story that is explainable only through an all-powerful, holy, and gracious God. It was one of those rare moments in my career when I was literally at a loss for the right words as I attempted to share my day with my wife and my son.

It began with my helping a young man who had just lost his father to an early death. He and I instantly

connected through our love for baseball. We also dis-
covered that his mother had worked for my son's college baseball coach. Was this connection and com-
monality just a coincidence? Was it just an irony that
my very next appointment was a twelve-year-old boy
who also entered my office wearing a baseball uniform
and was being raised by a single mom, as I was for
most of my childhood?

I spent the first part of the appointment with the
boy's mom, whom was not in her usual good spirits.
She began crying as she told me she had lost her job
and could not afford to buy her son a new pair of baseball pants, as his were ragged and full of holes. She also
explained that she was proud that he had been selected to the community all-star team but that she could
not afford the fee. She really began to be emotional as
she told me that her mom had given her fifteen dollars
to buy needed groceries.

During my time with this boy in my office, I attempted to encourage him by telling him about another young man his age who had been to my house
who was also raised by a single mom in a poor neighborhood without a lot of extras. I encouraged him to
watch the NBA draft that night on television as this

other young boy, who was now a twenty-three-year-old and was predicted to be in the top ten picks of the NBA draft.

As he sat there with a Boston Red Sox jersey and ball cap, I encouraged him to practice hard and play hard all the time as there might be a Boston Red Sox MLB scout watching him play someday. He left my office, as it was the end of the appointment, and went to the restroom to finish getting dressed for his baseball practice.

The next part of this story is nothing short of divine. My next appointment was a man in his early sixties who passed the twelve-year-old boy on his way into my office. This older gentleman was wearing a Boston Red Sox baseball cap! I couldn't believe it. We were in Ohio.

We quickly devised a plan for him to play the role of a professional baseball scout. You should have seen the eyes of the young boy light up. We all enjoyed the moment for a while, and then I shared the truth that he was not really a professional baseball scout. I again encouraged a young boy to play hard as there someday might be a real professional baseball scout watching him play.

By the end of my time with this elderly gentleman, he had given me money to give to the boy's mom to buy him some new baseball pants as well as some extra money that she could use for other needs like groceries. The spirit of giving had boosted this elderly man's mood.

I could not wait to tell of this miracle story, so I immediately called my wife only to get her voicemail. I then drove out of my way to my son's college house and was surprised to find him home. I eagerly told him of God's divine intervention in my office, and my son proceeded to tell me of a big bag in his closet at my home full of baseball uniforms, batting gloves, bats, and other used baseball items still in good shape that he had outgrown. "Give it all to him," he told me.

I felt like Santa Claus on Christmas morning showing up at this kid's doorstep. With his mom in tears and a smile as big as the state of Texas on this kid's face, I gave him the baseball stuff and his mom the money from an anonymous donor.

PRINCIPLE FOR LIVING:

It is always more blessed to give than to receive.

WEEK TWENTY-NINE

Whoever wants to be first must be your slave.

(Matthew 20:27)

SO, YOU WANT TO BE GREAT?

In August 1998 my family had bowed our heads at the dinner table as we have done so many times before. Oh, sure--my wife or I could easily lead our family in a prayer of thanksgiving for the food we were about to eat. But as I said before, we would rather hear a child's prayer any day of the week.

On that date my son, Kyler, at age seven, began thanking the Lord for the food. He also said in his prayer, "Thank You, Jesus, that my mom and dad help people."

My wife is undoubtedly in my mind one of the greatest physical therapy assistants the world has ever known. Her specialty is the geriatric population. She falls in love with her elderly patients and treats every one of them as if they were her grandparents. All my children have seen her in action. Kyler knew that his dad was a licensed professional counselor and life coach and that I was in the business of pointing people to the truth, both scientific as well as scriptural truth. But don't get me wrong--despite all this, there are many missed opportunities for my wife and me to help people.

Do you remember when the disciples were having a friendly debate surrounding the issue of who was the greatest? I'm sure they were discussing things like bank accounts, investment portfolios, sizes of homes and acreage, numbers of cars (chariots in those days) and on and on the discussion could go. Jesus stepped into the scene and gently explained to them that they were all wrong. For, you see, it is true: he who dies with the most toys does *not* win! Jesus says, "The greatest among you will be your servant" (Matthew 23:11). Let me assure you that people are always more important than the process.

Who in your life are you currently serving? Who do you know needs you to come alongside them and serve them? Albert Sweitzer said, "Those who have found true happiness are those who have found how to serve others." It doesn't matter what you do for a vocation--there are people in your life such as coworkers, immediate family members, extended family members, neighbors, community members, and others you can serve.

Let's be intentional about finding those in our sphere of influence we can serve. Perhaps someday it may not be necessarily our children who bow their heads and thank God above that we help people. It will be the Father of all fathers saying, "Well done, good and faithful servant!" (Matthew 25:21).

PRINCIPLE FOR LIVING:

Greatness equals servitude in God's eyes.

WEEK THIRTY

*In the beginning was the Word, and the Word
was with God, and the Word was God. He was with God
in the beginning. Through him all things were made;
without him nothing was made that has been made.*
(John 1:1-3)

*In the past God spoke to our ancestors
through the prophets at many times and in various
ways, but in these last days he has spoken to us by his
Son, whom he appointed heir of all things, and
through whom also he made the universe.*
(Hebrews 1:1-2)

*The fool says in his heart, "There is no God."
They are corrupt, their deeds are vile; there is no one who*

*does good. The L*ORD *looks down from
heaven on all mankind to see if there are any
who understand, any who seek God. All have turned
away, all have become corrupt; there is no one
who does good, not even one. Do all these evildoers
know nothing? They devour my people as though
eating bread; they never call on the L*ORD*. But there
they are, overwhelmed with dread, for God is present in
the company of the righteous.*

(Psalm 14:1-5)

AND SOME SAY THERE IS NO GOD

Our family was on a mini-vacation in the beautiful mountains of Beckley, West Virginia. We were spending three or four days with some very good friends of ours whitewater rafting in the New River Gorge.

After experiencing some of the best whitewater in the country, we pulled off to the side of the river to rest our arms and enjoy the beauty of God's creation. The river guide had pointed us to a trail that led to a waterfall. As we started off on the trail, my energetic children led the pack up the path. Some other river rafters had pulled off to the side to follow the path to the waterfall as well.

As we rounded the bend in the woods and could hear the waterfall, my son, who was thirteen years old at the time, rushed forward to see this magnificent waterfall. Kyler left the pack and ran back to those of us who took a little bit more energy to get up the hill and around the path. He then said something very profound. He looked at the waterfall, pointed, looked back at me, and said, "You see that waterfall, Dad?"

I said to him, "Yes I see it. It's magnificent."

Then Kyler said, "And some say there is no God."

Scripture tells us that God's creation points to Him (Romans 1:20). It is indeed hard to believe that some see a waterfall, a sunset over the ocean, the Grand Canyon, the birth of a baby--and still conclude that there is no Creator to this creation.

I am so grateful that we have raised our children to see God's handiwork in His creation and that at the young age of thirteen our son was reporting back to his parents that there is a God who created not only the beautiful waterfall but you and me as well.

PRINCIPLE FOR LIVING:

All creation points to a Creator.

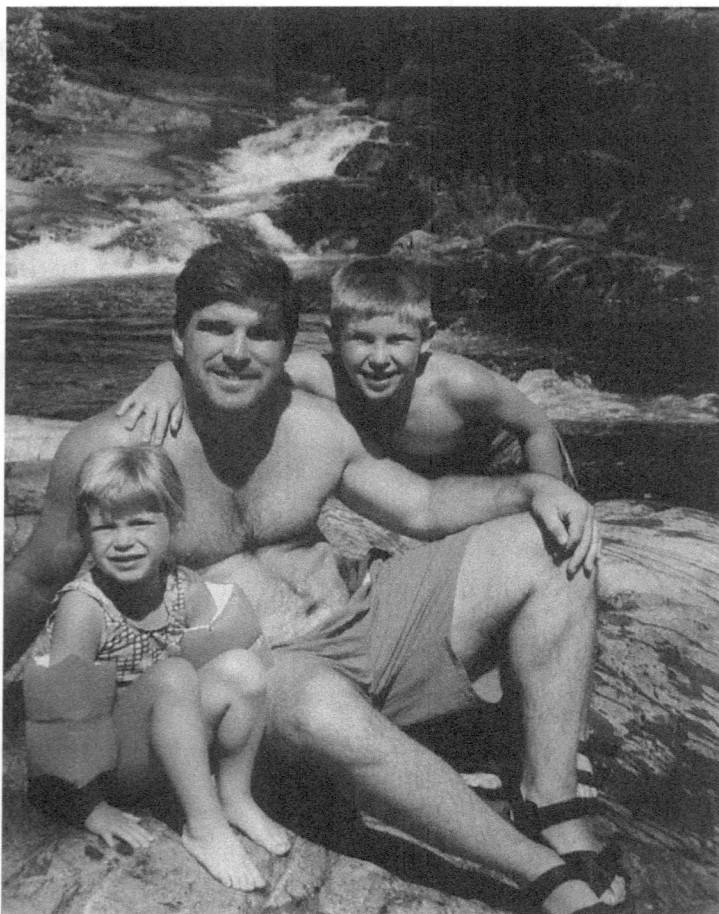

McKala, Tim, and Kyler in Canada

WEEK THIRTY-ONE

Ask and it will be given to you; seek and you will find;
knock and the door will be opened to you. For everyone
who asks receives; the one who seeks finds; and to the
one who knocks, the door will be opened.

(Matthew 7:7-8)

SEEK AND YOU WILL FIND

I have had the privilege of crisscrossing our country to speak to audiences of all sizes, including youth groups in camp settings. On one particular summer I was invited to travel to the upper peninsula of Michigan to share with a couple hundred students on the topic of student leadership.

After a twelve-hour drive, Stacy and I and our two kids were exhausted from our travels. After sharing with the students and their leaders in the opening session, we put our kids down for what we hoped to be a good night's rest. Stacy and I were on two rather uncomfortable bunk beds, but it really didn't matter because we were so exhausted that we could have slept on concrete that particular night.

As you well know, children are not nearly as picky about where they sleep. McKala was just an infant, so she had been tucked away in a portable crib for the evening. What was about to happen has left a mark upon our memory banks and hearts forever. At about 2:45 AM I awoke to a noise. After questioning myself–"Was I dreaming or just hearing things?"–I abruptly said to my wife, who was half-awake now, "Did you hear that?"

"I think I heard Kyler hollering my name." As only a loving mother can, Stacy went from being half-asleep to being very much wide awake. She quickly rolled over to hopefully feel Kyler's body tucked away in the sleeping bag. The sleeping bag was empty. I immediately flipped on a light only to notice that the door to our room was wide open. Do you think she and I thought to be modest at a camp filled with young Christian teenagers and their leaders? Absolutely not! We both tore out of the room heading in what we thought was the direction of his little voice. I frantically woke the entire camp hollering his name.

Yes, the story has a happy ending in that I found him wandering the campground by the camp lake looking for his mom and dad at 2:45 in the morning. He had awakened in the middle of the night and had sleepwalked out into the dark of the night to look for and holler for his parents after waking up in a strange place.

It's hard to describe your feelings and emotions once you find your four-year-old son walking by a lake in the middle of the night. Let's just be honest and say it was a tangled ball of emotions going through our minds. We both assured him that he was safe and assured him that we would not leave him. Man, did I underestimate those words from my wife! It took me an hour and a half to get around the barricade my wife built around the door as I was scheduled to go speak to the students at the morning session. We're happy to report to you that we can now look back and laugh about this incident.

So, what's the lesson to be learned? Kyler was desperately seeking for the presence of the two people who love him most and make him feel safe and secure—his mother and father. So it is with you and me: we seek for the One who promised never to leave us nor forsake us. He promised never to leave us alone, even in difficult times. We seek for the presence of the high and mighty One who can cause us to feel safe and secure in the midst of our dark nights.

Jesus himself said, "If you seek for the truth, you will find the truth." That truth is found in a person, and that person is Jesus Christ himself. I hope and pray that you have sought to find the Lord, and I hope you realize that when you find Him and commit your life to Him, He promises never to leave you or forsake you during the deepest, darkest hours of your life.

Principle for Living:

Seek for the truth in the person of
Jesus Christ. If you feel distant from God,
you left Him--for He will never leave you.

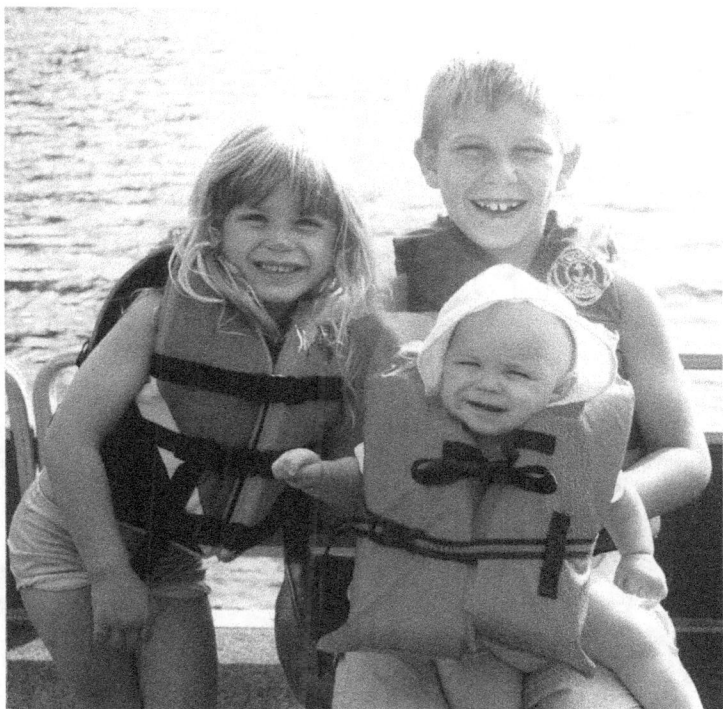

McKala, Kyler, and Kaleigh on a pontoon in Canada

WEEK THIRTY-TWO

*Which of these three do you think was a
neighbor to the man who fell into the hands of robbers?"
The expert in the law replied, "The one who had mercy
on him." Jesus told him, "Go and do likewise".*
(Luke 10:36-37)

LOVING THE UNLOVABLE

Kaleigh no doubt is my child with a gold-en heart. She has many times amazed her mother and me at how soft her heart is toward the un-lovable. One day after school she approached me and asked if I knew a specific classmate of hers. Since I had been very involved in our local school system, I in fact did know of this particular student. Kaleigh proceeded to tell me that this classmate would sit in the lunch-room alone. She had an unkempt appearance, and Kaleigh knew that this child came from a single-parent home and had a very rough home life.

She proceeded to tell me that all of God's creation is good and then informed me that she asked this classmate to come sit at her table. My heart melts now as I write this story, just as it did the day she told it to me. She also told me that she took some heat from her other classmates who were already sitting at her table on a regular basis for asking this unlovely classmate to sit with them.

How proud can a father be? Kaleigh had learned a life lesson and was teaching her dad that all of God's children matter and that we should go out of our way to love and be kind to the unlovely. It is easy for you and me to befriend the popular, rich, athletic, and good-looking. If you study the life of the greatest man to ever walk the face of the earth, you will find that He too hung around and befriended the unlovely.

Who do you know in your sphere of influence who needs a kind word, needs to be simply acknowledged, needs a pat on the back, and needs you to love him or her? All of the stories in this book surround life lessons learned from my children. Only two stories include other children. Both are, undoubtedly, supernatural life lessons. One of these is a story of how God taught me, and my entire family, a life lesson about love, and the power of love, that we will never forget.

I was working with a family who was having some difficulty with their mentally challenged son. Let's call him, Jay. Jay was a rather large, African American 16-year-old boy, who had the mental age of a 3 1/2-year-old. Since I knew that a 3 1/2-year-old can learn, I began to teach this young man to change his behavior by programming his mind with positive statements surrounding the behavior change his parents were hoping to see. I had developed a deep bond with this boy, too lengthy to explain in this short story. I told Jay to repeat after me, as I had done in previous sessions. I was going to attempt to have him say, "I will listen to, and obey my parents." I started, "I will," and then I paused for him to repeat those two words after me, before I continued with the rest of the statement. Jay looked at me with his big eyes and said, "I," and then he paused before continuing to say, "I love you, Dr. King." Needless to say, I was completely silent as I was overwhelmed at his imperative statement.

Just maybe, I was learning what unconditional love from another human being was like. Even with Jay's mental handicap, he was able to receive and give this powerful thing called love.

As a professional counselor, I can't begin to tell you the number of stories I have heard where a life was saved as a result of another human being paying attention to the needs of the unlovely. Let me challenge you as you read this story to keep your eyes open, and more importantly your heart open, to reach out and love on the unlovely.

PRINCIPLE FOR LIVING:

See others through the eyes of their Creator.

WEEK THIRTY-THREE

I want to know Christ--yes, to know the power
of his resurrection and participation in his sufferings,
becoming like him in his death.
(Philippians 3:10)

SO, YOU WANT TO HAVE A SUPERPOWER?

On the morning of Thursday July 14, 2005, my daughter Kaleigh was telling me about watching a cartoon and the special powers the cartoon characters had for getting rid of monsters. She made a very pointed statement that she wished she had such special powers.

My reply to my four-year-old was that you can have a power greater than those of the cartoon characters. Her eyes lit up and she replied with hope, "I can?"

I then proceeded to tell her that the same power that raised Jesus from the grave after He died on the Cross is available to those of us who believe in God's Son.

Kaleigh said, "Daddy, I want to have that superpower, so I'm going to pray a lot."

Man, do I ever hope that all my kids seek the Lord often through the power of prayer. Her little mind then switched to becoming a princess, and she asked me if I wanted to see her skate in her princess outfit.

"Of course," I said, and she scurried off to put on her princess outfit and her slippery slippers that glide across the kitchen floor.

PRINCIPLE FOR LIVING:

You can tap into a power far greater
than any power on earth.

WEEK THIRTY-FOUR

(Labor Day)

He chose to be mistreated along with
the people of God rather than to enjoy the
fleeting pleasures of sin.
(Hebrews 11:25)

CHORES ARE A BLAST!

God is very clear about the value of hard work. Stacy and I have not been completely successful in imparting all of God's values to our children, but this is one where I believe we did a great job. Since our children were knee-high to a grasshopper, they shared in household chores. My son, Kyler, actually joked one time that as soon as he was delivered as a newborn in the hospital, his mother and father handed him a chore list!

One summer afternoon I heard a commotion on the back of our duplex deck. As I approached the back door that led out onto our deck, I overheard Kyler, who was then six years old, doing one of the best sales jobs I've ever heard on his neighborhood friend. He was selling him on the point of how fun it is to clean up dog messes off the deck. You see, this was one of the chores that my wife and I delegated to our young son. I don't know if this is something I need to be proud of, but Kyler was successful. He convinced his neighborhood friend to grab a plastic bag and shovel and help him clean up the dog messes off our deck.

How my son convinced his buddy that cleaning up dog messes was fun has yet to be determined. My mind immediately went to the scripture that admonishes us to realize that sin is fun for a season (Hebrews 11:25). According to an old saying, you can play with fire only so long until you get burned. And yet another is that you can roll around with the pigs for only so long until you start smelling like a pig.

The archenemy is pretty crafty. He makes sin look enticing, smell enticing, feel enticing, and it appears to be fun. The truth of the matter is that sin can indeed be fun--but *only for a season.* Unfortunately, as a professional counselor I have been to funerals of young teenagers and young adults whose sin escapades ended in a parent's worst nightmare. They may have had a good time partying or being sexually active, but their sin ended in a tragic car crash or death from a dreaded disease like AIDS.

As loving parents, we should all strive to admonish our children of the enticing temptations, of the evil one who wants to devour them like a lion (1 Peter 5:8). A battle rages daily between good and evil, and the victor gets your child's mind. Please make sure that your children are aware of what's right and wrong according to God and His Word.

Principle for Living:

Sin is fun only for a season.

WEEK THIRTY-FIVE

Praise the L<small>ORD</small>. Praise God in his sanctuary;
praise him in his mighty heavens. Praise him for his acts
of power; praise him for his surpassing greatness.
Praise him with the sounding of the trumpet, praise him
with the harp and lyre, praise him with timbrel
and dancing, praise him with the strings and pipe,
praise him with the clash of cymbals, praise him
with resounding cymbals. Let everything that has
breath praise the L<small>ORD</small>. Praise the L<small>ORD</small>.
(Psalm 150:1-6)

PRAISING JESUS REALLY WORKS

I t was early fall and the weather was gorgeous. Stacy, Kyler, and I had traveled to some friends of ours who live in Wooster, Ohio. Across from their home is a cornfield where I decided to put my three-and-a half-year-old son on my shoulders and take a walk. Of course, I had another motive in that I love the outdoors and hunting whitetail deer. I thought I might look for some deer signs as I walked along the edge of the woods.

After lugging the little guy for quite a way, I decided to take him off my shoulders and let him get some exercise as well. As he held onto two fingers on my hand, we began walking down a row in the cornfield. While we were walking he looked up at me and said, "Daddy, guess what."

I replied, "What, Kyler?"

"Praising Jesus really works."

I asked Kyler, who was obviously in deep thought, "How do we praise Jesus?"

His answer was matter-of-fact and immediate. "We praise Jesus when we walk with Him and talk with Him and He tells me that I am His own."

These are paraphrased words from a song we had sung in church many times. It is this God who left all His glory to become like you and me and to feel as you and I do. It is this God who gave His only Son to die on a Cross the cruelest death that one could ever die.

From the mouth of a babe--my babe, my son--came some powerful words of truth. You see, praising Jesus really does work. Luke 19:10 tells us that if we praise the Lord we will understand our own purpose, privileges, and responsibilities. When was the last time you just paused to praise Jesus? Won't you take a walk through the proverbial cornfield today and allow Him to walk with you and talk to you and tell you once again that you are His own.

PRINCIPLE FOR LIVING:

Praising Jesus really works in mighty ways.

Kyler petting a deer

WEEK THIRTY-SIX

Jesus wept.

(John 11:35)

A SUPERNATURAL SOLO

Do you know the shortest Scripture verse of the entire Bible? I'm amazed at the many people who do not know the answer to this question. It is found in the Book of John, chapter 11 and verse 35. It simply says, "Jesus wept."

All human beings are created with tear ducts, one of whose purposes is for crying. Even bigger rough and tough men have these tear ducts. I am telling you that the tears did flow as my family grieved the loss of my mother when she passed away. She was a great wom-

an and modeled love to all. What I'm about to share
in the following sentences is one of those moments
when a father's chest is puffed out and he is one of the
proudest parents on the face of the earth.

I had the privilege of honoring my mother by
speaking at her funeral. I asked my children and the
rest of my mom's grandchildren if they wanted to par-
ticipate by reading a scripture or writing something
about Grandma. My youngest daughter, Kaleigh, surprised her mother and me when she--at the age of ten-
-asked if she could sing a song at the funeral. She wrote
the lyrics and put a melody to the song completely by
herself.

Kaleigh stepped up to the microphone and just like
an angel moved every tear duct in the audience to perform. The lyrics to this song are as follows:

It's okay to cry;
It's okay to say goodbye.
Woo oh, woo oh.
It's so hard and I'm so scared.
Woo oh, woo oh.
God is glad and we're so sad.
Woo oh, woo oh.
I'll pray for you; I just knew.
Woo oh, woo oh.

Oh. she's in a better place;
I think we solved the case.
I love her--I'm so sure.
Woo oh, woo oh.
It's okay to cry;
It's okay to say goodbye.
It's all okay.

If crying was something Jesus did, it's something we should do. It's okay to cry. What is it that you have never fully grieved over?

PRINCIPLE FOR LIVING:

Tears are God's language.

They speak when words are inept.

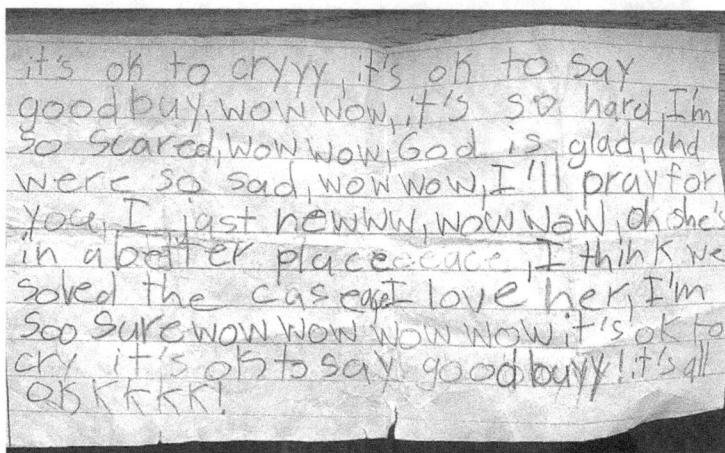

Kaleigh's lyrics

Kaleigh

WEEK THIRTY-SEVEN

Your word is a lamp for my feet, a light on my path.
(Psalm 119:105)

WHOSE SHOES ARE YOU FILLING?

One of my favorite things to do early on in our marriage was to drive to southern Ohio and spend the weekend with Stacy's Aunt Ruth. I could tell stories for a long time about life lessons learned while in the country at Aunt Ruth's.

Kyler was eight and McKala was three when McKala decided to put on her mommy's shoes and attempt to walk over to her mom and Aunt Ruth. After about four slow but sure steps, it happened. Her little feet and legs could not lift and step in her mother's shoes, which were obviously too big for her little feet. After a couple of jiggles and wiggles and attempting to save her nose, she began to stumble and fall face first.

It was not the biggest traumatic event by any means that has happened in our children's lives nor the most traumatic event that ever took place in southern Ohio at Aunt Ruth's, and yet there's certainly a life lesson to be learned. So many young children grow up and try to put themselves in the shoes of another individual. They're often in this comparison game that leads to envy, anger, and low self-worth. We have taught our children that they are incredible, unique, special creations of God, that there is only one of them, and that God has a special plan for their lives. We want our children to grow up and walk in their own shoes and to be themselves. We want them to carve out their own path and live out their own faith, to follow the purpose God has cut out for them.

You and I would do well not to attempt to try to be somebody else other than the person God created us to be. I'm reminded that our life here on earth truly ramps up when we strive to put our feet into the shoes of Jesus Christ and then to follow the path He has carved out for us as individuals.

PRINCIPLE FOR LIVING:

Follow in the footsteps of Christ.

Tim holding McKala

WEEK THIRTY-EIGHT

When you walk, they [your father's command
and your mother's teaching] will guide you;
when you sleep, they will watch over you; when you
awake, they will speak to you.
(Proverbs 6:22)

THEY ALL GROW UP

One of the most potent drugs in our culture is the drug of busyness. It has been said that "busy" stands for "being under Satan's yoke"! If you are reading this short story right now, I plead with you-- do not allow yourself to be so busy that you miss your children growing up.

One fall day my daughter Kaleigh and I were lying on the hammock during our family vacation. This was nothing out of the ordinary other than I began noticing the curls in my three-year-old daughter's hair. I began thinking about how her childlike, stunning, cute little face would someday grow up into the face of a beautiful young woman. The Scripture says, "Train up a child in the way he should go: and when he is old, he will not depart from it (Proverbs 22:6, KJV).

Both of my girls and probably your little girl as well like to play dress-up. I can remember McKala and her friend Taylor playing dress-up at our friend's house. It is a reminder to us parents that our children may aspire to be like us. I hope that all moms reading this story will read Proverbs 31 and begin modeling the behavior of a Proverbs 31 woman. It's difficult to read that chapter of the Bible and not begin praying for our daughters to grow up to be that kind of woman.

So, as I was reminded that day on the hammock, let me remind you today that the cute little curls in your daughter's hair and the big blue eyes on her face and the pudgy little cheeks will change, and she will grow up to be a young lady. Let us commit to raising more little girls to grow up to be Proverbs 31 women.

PRINCIPLE FOR LIVING:

Instill the precepts of God on your children's hearts.

McKala in her senior year of high school

WEEK THIRTY-NINE

I will praise you as long as I live,
and in your name, I will lift up my hands.
(Psalm 63:4)

AMERICAN IDOL OR JESUS AS IDOL?

Our family has never claimed to be gifted in the area of music or singing; however, we have grown up enjoying different genres of music and singing various songs in church. We are capable of singing melody and occasionally being in tune for a harmonious part. I certainly have learned lifelong lessons from my children as I have listened to their little vocal chords belt out songs filled with truth.

One of my favorite memories of my children was when my son was teaching his little sister McKala the hand motions of the song "Lord, I Lift Your Name on

High." During that time of our family's life that song became the family favorite, telling the good news of the gospel of Christ. Of course, there are motions that make the song more interesting, but more importantly the motions drive the message of the song more deeply into the recesses of our minds and our hearts.

Envision the words and the motions coming from a six-year-old and two-year-old. The only word to describe what I saw and heard is *priceless!*

So, what's the life lesson to be learned? Do you truly comprehend the essence of the Christian message that the God of the universe who owns everything chose to give His only Son to die on a cross and to be buried in a borrowed tomb and to rise to life on the third day so that you and I may have eternal life in heaven? It is indeed one amazing story of grace. It is no doubt a game-changer, a life-changer, and most importantly an eternity-changer.

I hope you hear the words of a six-year-old and a two-year-old, that we together someday might sing this song of good news and praise to the Father of all fathers together in heaven for all eternity.

PRINCIPLE FOR LIVING:

The person you talk about the most will be the person your children will aspire to be like.

WEEK FORTY

No one is like you, Lᴏʀᴅ; you are great,
and your name is mighty in power.
(Jeremiah 10:6)

WHO IS THAT MAN?

In July 1996 my nephew was over at my house playing with his cousin--my son, Kyler. I was preparing another message for a group of young people for a student leadership conference. There was a music video on television, and an artist named Carmen was singing a song entitled "Great God," which includes the words "He is a great God." I overheard my nephew, who was age five, singing, "He is a great guy."

Kyler, who was much more familiar with the song and video, immediately corrected his cousin and said,

"No, He is a great *God*, not just a great *guy*." I sat in my chair and chuckled at the mix-up of words from my nephew, and I even chuckled a little more when my son was so quick to be corrective.

I found myself whispering a little prayer that these two little guys would grow up to know that God is not just God but that He is a great and good God. I also found myself praying that God would keep them from vain philosophies of life that teach that Jesus was just a great teacher, just a great leader, or just a great prophet. You see, it is our faith and belief that Christ Jesus was God brought into the earth in the form of a man, the greatest man to ever walk the face of the earth, the God-man. Jesus of Christmas and Easter is truly beyond a great "guy." He is a great God.

PRINCIPLE FOR LIVING:

Your view about God is the most
important thing about you.

WEEK FORTY-ONE

The word of God is alive and active.
Sharper than any double-edged sword, it penetrates
even to dividing soul and spirit, joints and marrow;
it judges the thoughts and attitudes of the heart.
(Hebrews 4:12)

YOU CAN BE A SURGEON

On one cool October evening my family sat down to engage in the October activity of pumpkin-carving. I never claimed to be a professional pumpkin-carver, and maybe that's why I began carving my pumpkin with a butter knife. After cutting outside the lines, just as I colored outside the lines when I was a kid, I finally got frustrated and said to my wife,

"Stacy get me the sharpest knife we have in our kitchen drawer, please."

You see, my intention was to be a meticulous surgeon on this pumpkin. We certainly are a competitive family, and I wanted my pumpkin to look the best in the neighborhood. While my wife was retrieving a sharper knife for me, Kyler in his childlike faith and wisdom piped up and said, "Dad, Jesus is the sharpest." Kyler had just heard a lesson in his school about the Word of God being Jesus.

John 1:1 says, "In the beginning was the Word, and the Word was with God, and the Word was God." Kyler also had learned the scripture verse that says, "The word of God is quick, and powerful, and sharper than any two-edged sword, piercing even to the dividing asunder of soul and spirit, and of the joints and marrow, and is a discerner of the thoughts and intents of the heart" (Hebrews 4:12, KJV).

His little mind had connected the dots, and that is why he was letting me know that Mom was not going to retrieve out of our kitchen drawer the sharpest knife--because the sharpest sword/knife is found from Genesis chapter 1 to Revelation chapter 22. It is the sharp truth that we need to hide in our hearts and to share with our children every opportunity we get.

PRINCIPLE FOR LIVING:

It is the Word of God that has the power to change us.

Tim and Kaleigh at the pumpkin patch

Cousins at the pumpkin patch

WEEK FORTY-TWO

As every man hath received the gift,
even so minister the same one to another,
as good stewards of the manifold grace of God.
(1 Peter 4:10)

OPEN YOUR PRESENTS

As I write this chapter it just happens to be the month of December, the month when children look forward to opening presents at Christmas time and when we rejoice in the greatest gift ever given to humanity, the baby Jesus.

It's also a time where my two daughters and I inevitably end up in one of my least favorite places on the face of the earth--the mall. Of course, my daughters do not like to go shopping; I have learned that they like to go *buying*. Kaleigh on one of her "just because" home-made cards to dad writes, "My dad is the best becus [because] he hunts dears [deer] and loves me and be-cus [because] he buys me Presis [presents]."

The Word of God tells us that God gives all of us presents. These come to us in the way of abilities, tal-ents, and opportunities (1 Peter 4:10). Buying your children gifts is a good opportunity to teach them that what matters most in life is the intangible things. not the tangible gifts we all open at birthday parties and/or Christmas.

Maybe you're not aware of these presents that God has given you. Maybe you feel that God passed you up when He gave out these presents. Let me assure you that He did not pass you up. You have gifts, abilities, and talents. My question to you is "Do you know what these gifts are, and are you using those gifts for the glory and honor of Christ?" (1 Corinthians 10:31).

PRINCIPLE FOR LIVING:

Use your talents to honor God.

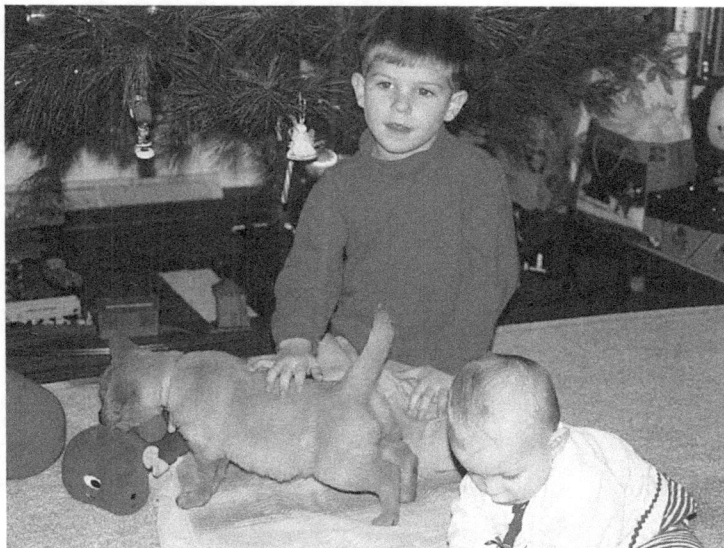

Kyler and McKala getting a puppy for Christmas

WEEK FORTY-THREE

I can do all this through him who gives me strength.

(Philippians 4:13)

FORTUNE COOKIES CAN LEAD
TO DEEP TRUTH

One of the highlights of the week for my family is going out to lunch after attending church together. Of course, an organized family must come up with a strategy of who gets to pick the restaurant where the family will eat. It never ceases to amaze me how one family can have such a diverse array of taste buds. There have been many Sundays I felt as if I should turn the car around and go back to church so that my family could work out their conflict of a restaurant choice.

On one Sunday--and I don't recall which family member won the choice of restaurant that week--we ended up at a Chinese restaurant. A Chinese restaurant can be a good place for diverse pallets, because they usually have a wide variety of food, not just Chinese dishes. One of the highlights of eating, of course, is finding out which family member is going to win millions of dollars according to his or her fortune cookie!

On one particular Sunday my wife opened up her fortune cookie and read her fortune to the family. It got the usual eye roll from me. I then read my own fortune to the family, which was a word of advice to be kind to all and that kindness would return tenfold.

What happened next at our lunch table is the life lesson in this short story that I hope resonates in your heart and mind forever. Our son, Kyler, who had just turned five and was not a proficient reader as of yet, spoke up and said, "Daddy, do you want to know what *my* fortune cookie says?" I gave his mother one of those proverbial eye looks that she interpreted as "This is going to be good." Kyler then sat up tall--well, as tall as he could--and said, "My fortune cookie says 'In Christ alone.'"

Do you ever have one of those moments at the dinner table when you're tempted to say something but you know silence is the best choice? Stacy and I sat for a short period of silence, and then she spoke up and said, "That's right, Kyler--in Christ alone all things are possible."

This was the year that Kyler had received a Dallas Cowboys jersey and a Dallas Cowboys football helmet as gifts. Kyler and I watched a video including a Christian music artist who had been quoted by Frank Reight, the NFL quarterback who had led the largest comeback from a halftime deficit to lead his team to an NFL victory. The title of the music video was "In Christ Alone."

I hope you're choosing to feed your children's minds with good songs, poems, stories, and, of course, the Scriptures. I hope your "future fortune" is inclusive of Christ in every facet.

PRINCIPLE FOR LIVING:

All things are possible with Christ.

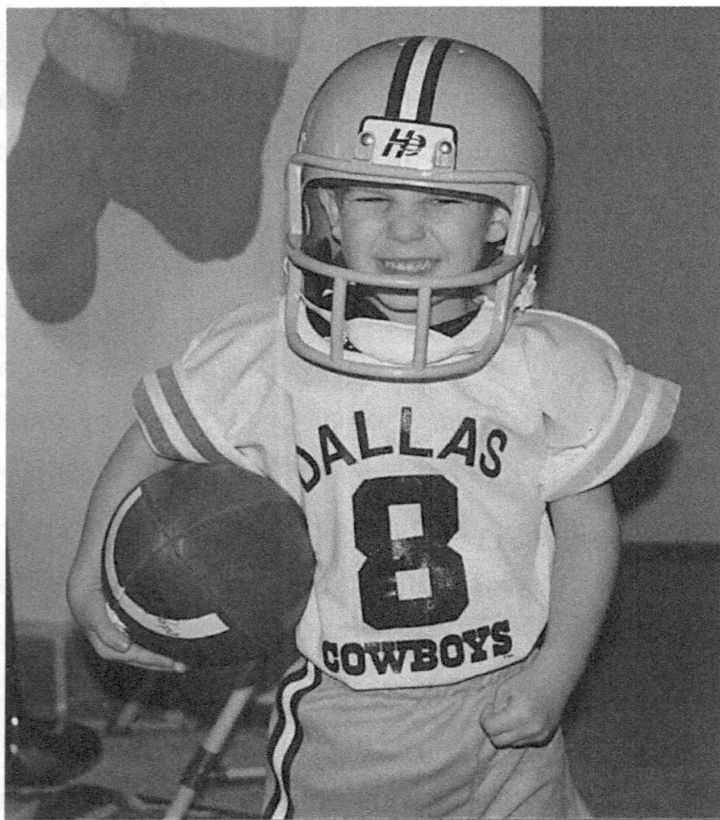

Kyler in his Cowboys uniform

WEEK FORTY-FOUR

If you are offering your gift at the altar
and there remember that your brother or sister
has something against you, leave your gift there in
front of the altar. First go and be reconciled to them;
then come and offer your gift.
(Matthew 5:23-24)

WHY IS IT SO TOUGH?

O ne of the facts of human nature is that we are born into a self-centered selfishness. This reality makes it difficult in the parenting process to teach children to apologize. Why is it for many of us that it is so difficult to say the words "I'm sorry" and "I was wrong"?

Kyler was seven years old and his little sister McKala was three, and it was one of those days when sibling conflict was in the air. McKala had picked up one of her big brother's toys, and he was having none of it. The battle was on. Things were getting somewhat heated until dad showed up on the scene.

Being the expert in these crisis situations, I thought I would use the "WWJD" (What would Jesus do?) approach. I said to Kyler exactly that: "What would Jesus do?"

Kyler's prompt response was not what I expected. He replied in a harsh, frustrated tone, "Jesus would tell Sissy not to touch my toys."

Once I realized that the sin nature was alive and well, I changed my approach. I made Kyler apologize to his little sister. He initially made no eye contact with his sister, and his voice tone made it clear that he was not truly sorry for his actions as he simply said, "Sorry, Sissy," and began walking away. I proceeded to make him turn around and come back, look her in the eyes, and say that he was sorry with a different tone of voice.

You and I both know that a sincere apology comes from the heart. It is a heart issue. It is only when we realize that we are not living out the principles of God's truth that we can give a sincere, heartfelt apology for our wrong behavior.

As a professional counselor, I have seen my share of conflict in the office. It never ceases to amaze me how stubborn and prideful human beings can be. I am convicted myself as I write this short story. We--I--have to get better at living out this principle of truth.

The story of the prodigal son is a great example of this principle. When the wayward son came to his senses and lowered his pride, it is then that he came to his father and said, "I was wrong, I am sorry, and will you forgive me?"

I am pleased to say that as my children grew older, they learned to get along better. I often see them embrace, and I know they love each other. Make no mistake about it: our Creator intends for us to live in peace and harmony as much as possible. Let's commit today to doing better at owning responsibility for our wrong behavior and making peace with others.

PRINCIPLE FOR LIVING:

Take responsibility for your own behavior
and seek peace with others.

McKala and Kyler

WEEK FORTY-FIVE

(Thanksgiving)

Give thanks in all circumstances;
for this is God's will for you in Christ Jesus.
(1 Thessalonians 5:18)

HAVING A GOOD DAY?

How is your day going? Some would answer, "Good," and others would answer, "Bad." As I've mentioned in previous chapters, it is an absolute pleasure to hear children pray. Stacy and I made it a habit to pray with our children as we tucked them into bed for the evening. From a very young age McKala would begin her prayer as follows: "Thank You, Lord, for good this day." I am reminded of the principled truth that says, "This is the day which the Lord hath made; we will rejoice and be glad in it" (Psalm 118:24, KJV). Every time Stacy and I would hear little McKala pray at nighttime we would be reminded of that truth.

If we truly take the time to count our blessings and not focus on the day's problems, we would have an attitude of gratitude and be willing to say, "Thank You, Lord, for good this day."

PRINCIPLE FOR LIVING:

Choose to be thankful and rejoice in all things.

Kyler in his Pilgrim outfit

WEEK FORTY-SIX

As the deer pants for streams of water,
so my soul pants for you, my God.
(Psalm 42:1)

MY UTMOST FOR HIS HIGHEST

I will never forget going to my children's Christian school to watch their very first choir concert. It is almost comical to watch the younger grades look out into the audience to find their mom, dad, grandma, grandpa, or other loved ones. Beyond the humor are the deep truths that these little mouths can utter. The same scenario can happen when the mouths of babes open up to belt out a melody in the church setting.

My son's very first choir concert was titled "My Utmost for His Highest." What a deep truth and a deep prayer that should be on the heart and mind of every parent! I know it is true for Stacy and me. We long for God to hear and answer our prayer when we ask Him to help our children keep Him at the forefront of their priorities. We pray that they would long to have a deep, intimate relationship with the person of Jesus Christ, just as a thirsty man in the desert would long for a drink of water.

I remember Kyler singing a song at a church where I was a guest speaker. It alluded to this deep thirsting for relationship with God, stating, "As the deer panteth for the water so my soul longeth after You." Kyler was four years old at the time and was standing right beside his dad as he heard the song being sung by the music director and the people of the congregation. His little mind forgot that he was in church, and he began thinking he was in the woods deer hunting with his dad.

What happened next continues to bring me and everybody I tell the story a deep belly laugh. When the song leader and the congregation sang, "As the deer..." Kyler yelled out at the top of his little lungs, "Bang!"

His little mind figured that if the deer stopped to get a drink of water, it was a good time to harvest it. If you love hunting in the outdoors, you might have a tendency to agree with him.

While it is very clear that God has a sense of humor, it is also my prayer that my children long to know the person of Jesus Christ in a very intimate way and that the longing is so great that it surpasses the longing for a drink of water after days in a hot desert.

PRINCIPLE FOR LIVING:

Set your priorities--with God being first.

Kyler on far right

McKala in the middle holding doll

WEEK FORTY-SEVEN

Every good and perfect gift is from above,
coming down from the Father of the heavenly
lights, who does not change like shifting shadows.
(James 1:17)

A FUNNY TURKEY HARVEST

When Kaleigh was six years old she gave me a homemade birthday card that had a picture she drew of two people in a tree stand hunting turkeys. For any of the outdoorsmen and outdoorswomen reading this story, you know that you do not hunt turkeys from a tree stand.

I laughed out loud when I first opened up her card and saw the drawing. Scripture tells us that laughter is good medicine for our souls (Proverbs 17:22). Turkeys are associated with all the other good food we eat with family and friends on Thanksgiving Day. If you follow the weekly sequence in reading this book, it should now be around Thanksgiving time. The food we eat on Thanksgiving Day, as well as any other day, nourishes our bodies. We need to nourish both our spirit and our body. Thanksgiving time is an opportunity to teach our children that all good things come from above (James 1:17).

It's a time to teach our children that it's God who grows the fruits, vegetables, and meats we eat every day. It's an opportunity to teach that we are thankful not just for the food we eat on Thanksgiving Day but also for God's provision *every* day of our lives.

PRINCIPLE FOR LIVING:

All good things come from God.

Kaleigh's drawing

WEEK FORTY-EIGHT

About three in the afternoon Jesus cried out in a loud
voice, "Eli, Eli, lema sabachthani?" (which means
"My God, my God, why have you forsaken me?").
(Matthew 27:46)

UNBEARABLE PAIN

Can you imagine the pain that God the Father must have felt when He couldn't even look at His only begotten Son bearing the pain and sin of the world on the Cross? No human father will ever be able to grasp that feeling as we are human and God's Son died the cruelest death that any person has ever died.

I can remember when my son, Kyler, at the age of two gave me a little glimpse of what God the Fa-

ther must have felt on that day. He was having difficulty going to the bathroom, and his mom was con-
cerned to the point that we took him to the children's
hospital to have some testing done. The nurses were
trained professionals and knew that the dynamic of a
mother's love was too great to see her two-year-old
son strapped to a board like a mummy, so Mom was
asked to wait in the waiting room. Kyler was strapped
to a board so he would remain completely still during
the barium enema test that they were about to admin-
ister. To be honest, it was tough for a loving father to
watch as well.

The glimpse into our Heavenly Father's pain came
to me after the test was done. The nurses handed me
my son, who continued to exercise his little lungs with
an ear-piercing cry; then he put a death grip around
my neck, as though he planned to never let go. And
then--the nurses came back and said that the results of
the test were not conclusive and that they were going
to have to perform the test again.

Prying that two-year-old little boy off my neck and
handing him back to the nurses for a second round of
discomfort and pain was very, very tough. I received a
little glimpse of God the Father turning His gaze away

from His Son, Jesus, who was not only in physical pain but also in emotional and mental pain as well bearing the full weight of our sin, the world's sin, on the Cross. Because of His love, Jesus Christ bore my pain, your pain, and the world's pain.

PRINCIPLE FOR LIVING:

GRACE: God's Riches At Christ's Expense.

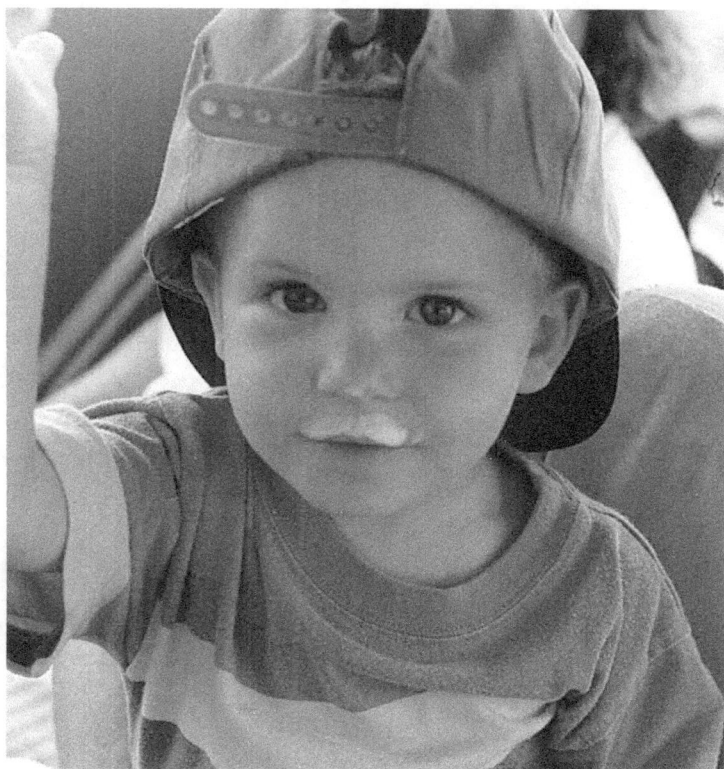

Kyler in New York

WEEK FORTY-NINE

*We love because he first loved us. Whoever
claims to love God yet hates a brother or sister is a
liar. For whoever does not love their brother and sister,
whom they have seen, cannot love God, whom they
have not seen. And he has given us this command:
Anyone who loves God must also
love their brother and sister.*

(1 John 4:19-21)

THE GREATEST GIFT OF ALL

Kaleigh writes in one of her homemade cards,
"Me and the best dad ever, Tim King. We do
everything together, like racing [She and I are in a go-

cart together]. He loves me, and I love him back. I love you so much."

When it is all said and done at the end of our life, the question is "How did you love God and people?" In Luke 10:27 we read about the importance of loving God with all our heart, soul, mind, and strength--and loving our neighbor as ourselves. Why? Because He first loved us (John 3:16).

Do you love God back by how you live your life? Stacy and I have fond memories of singing with our children, "Jesus loves me! This I know, for the Bible tells me so." What an incredible truth to live by!

PRINCIPLE FOR LIVING:

There is nothing you can do good to make
God love you more and nothing you can do bad to
make God love you less.

Kyler in Myrtle Beach

WEEK FIFTY

Even when we were with you,
we gave you this rule: "The one who is
unwilling to work shall not eat."
(2 Thessalonians 3:10)

WORK IS NOT A DIRTY WORD

McKala and Kaleigh write in one of their Father's Day cards to me, "Dear Dad, thank you for working hard for the family. We love you." As mentioned before, Stacy and I did teach our children to have a hard work ethic.

One evening when my wife had some friends over, somehow their conversation turned to the subject of child birthing. One of the ladies asked me what my response was when the nurses handed me my newborn son, Kyler, for the first time. Before I could respond, my son, who was eavesdropping in another room, said, "The first thing my dad did was hand me a chore list!" Not true--however, if it were true, the list would have been pretty short: eat, sleep, mess my diapers, and pee.

On a later occasion after having experienced the emotions of dropping our firstborn off at college, we were eventually faced with the process of dropping off our oldest daughter at college. Kaleigh, our youngest daughter, was extremely emotional hugging her big sister prior to our departing for home. McKala was embracing Kaleigh and attempting to console her with statements such as "I will come home on some weekends, and you can sometimes come stay here at college with me."

Kaleigh attempted to catch her breath and then said, "I'm not crying just because I'm going to miss you--I am crying because I am the only kid that has to go home to do all of the kids' chores."

Now I don't want you to think that my wife and I are slave-drivers, but one thing is for sure: God is very clear about a hard work ethic (2 Thessalonians 3:10). Stacy and I understood these principles of Scripture and taught our children to work hard and do their best.

Principle for Living:

God will bless us for hard work, and
there are negative consequences for being lazy.

WEEK FIFTY-ONE

(Christmas)

So, they hurried off and found Mary and Joseph, and the baby, who was lying in the manger. When they had seen him, they spread the word concerning what had been told them about this child, and all who heard it were amazed at what the shepherds said to them. But Mary treasured up all these things and pondered them in her heart. The shepherds returned, glorifying and praising God for all the things they had heard and seen, which were just as they had been told.

(Luke 2:16-20)

THE GREATEST STORY EVER TOLD!

We at the King household have a few traditions during the Christmas season. One of these involves taking turns reading the Christmas story on the morning of Christmas Day before opening up our gifts. My children have memorized the first twenty verses of Luke 2, which is Luke's account of the birth of Jesus Christ, the Christmas story.

If you've not noticed by now, I'm a dad who likes to tell stories. I'm always amazed at how Jesus taught through stories, called parables in the Scripture. It is this story, the Christmas story (as well as the Easter story), that motivates me to write. As a matter of fact, it is this story that motivates me to be a better parent. It is the Christmas story that gives us a reason and purpose to live and serve others while here on earth. To hear my respective children at an elementary age, quote those twenty verses from memory brings nothing less than pure joy to my wife and me.

Indeed, Luke 2:1-20 will always have a special meaning in the King household. Today I bring you great tidings of joy: A Savior has been born, and His name is Jesus.

Principle for Living:
Jesus is the reason for the season.
Never take Christ out of Christmas.

Kyler opening a Christmas present

WEEK FIFTY-TWO

(New Year's Eve)

*Do not store up for yourselves
treasures on earth, where moths and vermin
destroy, and where thieves break in and steal.*
(Matthew 6:19)

*Be alert and of sober mind. Your enemy
the devil prowls around like a roaring lion
looking for someone to devour.*
(1 Peter 5:8)

THE GRAND BATTLE

Fifty-one truths have entered the recesses of your brain if you have read this book in its entirety. I have saved one of the most sobering principled truths for last.

The end of the year is when family and friends come together to bring one year to a close and celebrate the ushering-in of a new year. Many times, my wife, children, and I would head out to join family and friends for a new year's party.

One particular year we played a game called "Dirty Santa" at the party, in which you can actually take your neighbor's gifts. The game can be pretty intense. At this particular New Year's party, I was in competition with the other players around table to win four box seats to a Cleveland Indians baseball game, which was one of the gifts on the table. The tickets were in somebody else's hand until I rolled doubles on the dice and snatched them from my upset neighbor. This is all part of the game, you see.

So, there I was with four box seat tickets in my hand to see my favorite professional baseball team, and the clock was winding down to bring an end to the game. You get to keep the gifts in your possession when the final buzzer goes off on the time clock.

Sure enough, the buzzer went off and I was holding four box seats to the ballgame. I was elated. I stood up on my chair and almost injured myself putting my arms up in the air like Rocky Balboa into a ceiling fan to celebrate that I had won one of the most prized gifts going around the table in this dirty Santa game.

It did not take me long to notice that the majority of our friends and family were on the floor laughing at me. I did not understand why they would not be high-fiving me, envious of me and celebrating with me. The reason became clear. The tickets I was holding in my hand were for last year's baseball season. They were bogus tickets.

I had given away legitimate gifts to keep fake tickets. I had been duped. I had been deceived.

What a great opportunity to teach my children a sobering truth! For all you parents who have read this book, you must understand that there is a grand battle between good (God) and evil (Satan), and it is sobering to understand that the victor of this battle gets your child's mind. Just as I had been deceived into believing that the Cleveland Indians tickets were real and that it was important for me to win them, the great deceiver, Satan himself, gets you and me as parents to focus our energy and effort on the temporary as opposed to the things that are eternal.

Let us together make a commitment in this new year that our focus and energy will be on using our gifts and talents to further the kingdom of God, to share Christ with people, and to disciple them to reach their full potential for Christ. Let's commit to lay up treasures in heaven, where moth and rust don't corrupt (Matthew 6:19). Let's not build our lives with wood, hay, and stubble, but let us choose to build with things that last for eternity with the gold, silver, and precious stone (1 Corinthians 3:12-13). For sure, let us commit to not missing out on learning all the truths and life lessons that the little professors in your household and mine are teaching us.

PRINCIPLE FOR LIVING:

Learn from the "little professors" --
we call them *children!*

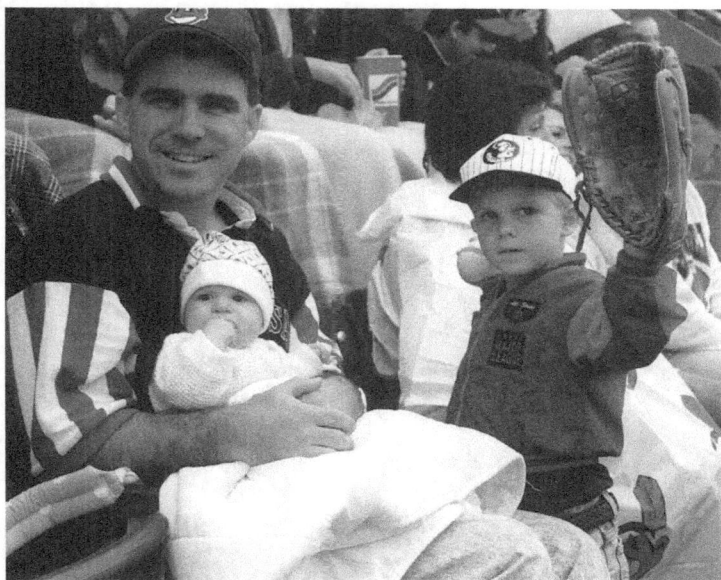

Tim holding McKala, and Kyler at a ball game

www.ingramcontent.com/pod-product-compliance
Lightning Source LLC
LaVergne TN
LVHW020055090426
835513LV00029B/1513